Franciscans in Urban Ministry

Ken Himes, O.F.M.

Edited by Roberta A. McKelvie, O.S.F.

Franciscans in Urban Ministry

Ken Himes, O.F.M.

Franciscan Institute Publications
St. Bonaventure University
St. Bonaventure, NY
2002

© The Franciscan Institute
St. Bonaventure University
St. Bonaventure, NY 14778
2002

The cover is adapted from a watercolor by Edith M. Cowles,
first published in *GIOTTO The Legend of St. Francis
as Depicted in the Assisi Frescoes*
(New York: E.P. Dutton and Co., Inc., 1931*)*

Library of Congress number
2002107218

ISBN number: 1-57659-182-4

Printed in the United States of America
BookMasters, Inc.
Mansfield, OH

Table of Contents

Introduction

Since the dawn of the Franciscan movement early in the thirteenth century, Franciscans have found themselves living and ministering in significant ways in the context of cities. This phenomenon continues to the present as Franciscans – seculars, sisters and friars – respond to the call to live and proclaim the Gospel of Jesus Christ in the world. The contemporary urban setting is still fertile ground within which people can live their "Franciscan" vocation.

Franciscan tradition, beginning with the life of Francis of Assisi himself, grounds itself squarely in an incarnational approach to life. The Word takes on human flesh and lives within the human condition. This truth fascinated Francis and motivated his entire being. Through the Incarnation he saw that God affirmed the goodness of all creation and desired to bring that goodness to completion in Jesus. Francis saw everything in creation as related to everything else and to God; it is this relatedness that gives meaning to everything. In the person of Jesus, Word made flesh, the Franciscan sees what it means to live and work in the world. In the language of Francis, everything is "brother," everything is "sister."

Living in the city was a newly emerging way of life at the time of Francis. Life for the early Franciscans was life in the city. The city was their world, the locus for living the incarnation, for proclamation, for evangelization, for uncovering meaning.

So the city is today. As in the time of the early Franciscans, city life is changing; it is being re-defined. Such change is part of the nature of what it means to be a city in a post-modern world. For example, currently, at least in cities in a North American context, we see things like:

- booming economies;
- accumulation of wealth in the hands of a relatively small number of people; (currently, in the United States, 1% of the population controls 45% of the wealth);
- resultant increases in discretionary income and a re-gentrification of previously neglected urban settings by newly wealthy younger people;
- shrinking real wages for people on the lower end of the wage scale and increasing numbers of "working poor";

1

- skyrocketing cost of housing and a lack of affordable housing for people on the lower end of the socio-economic scale;
- increasing numbers of homeless people;
- massive immigration, i.e., people to do the work, accompanied by linguistic, cultural, religious and racial differences;
- a changing definition of work because of new technologies;
- movement of unskilled jobs to locations overseas and away from urban settings due to increasing costs of land and labor;
- increasing transportation problems within and between cities;
- growing concerns about urban environments: air quality, water quality, the quality of food, aging infra-structures, waste disposal treatment, growing need for energy, urban "brown fields"; and
- new and ever-changing modes of communication based on new technologies.

With this backdrop, we see a growing rift between rich and poor people; the haves and the have-nots. There are clear differences between advantaged and disadvantaged people; educated and under-educated people; employed, under-employed, and unemployed people. All of these factors require on-going reconsideration of what it means to be socialized, to be fully human, in a particular concrete, current urban form. Consequently, an on-going tension exists for urban ministry as people involved in it seek to respond to such tremendous cultural, economic and social changes.

Our work in the current text is an attempt to examine this unique aspect of Franciscan life. Assuming that the lives of Francis and his early followers remain a credible model for engaging in a process of urban evangelization, we explore some salient features of the Franciscan story and consider some contemporary approaches to life and ministry in the city. Each of the essays in the book represents different, though complementary, urban concerns.

The Franciscan story is a human story, a story of flexibility and vulnerability, a story of preaching more by deeds than by words, a story of people who are highly transient, itinerant, ready to move with people on the move, with changing needs and within the changing realities of life. It is a movement that grounds evangelization on human dignity as the fundamental basis for human unity.

Consequently, the typical Franciscan urban ministry is not focused primarily on "parish" as a locus of activity, but rather on providing services that meet human needs and addressing justice-related issues. Franciscan ministry, including "preaching," a primary mode of ministry in the Franciscan heritage, is a style of engagement wherein the minister is brother/sister to the people encountered in the context of their daily lives. Such engagement does not necessarily happen within an ecclesial or even a specifically pastoral setting or institution. Rather, for the Franciscan, justice is simply face-to-face contact, standing with, standing beside the other because they embody the Christ. **Ministry is not a pastoral work; it is a way of living and being in the world with other people.** A Franciscan ministers, preaches, evangelizes, and leads primarily by living life well with others.

This volume contains a series of seven articles crafted to provide an overview of a Franciscan approach to urban life and ministry. The differing styles found among the essays reflect the varied backgrounds and vantage points of our authors. The book is the result of a seminar hosted by Holy Name Province of the Order of Friars Minor, but participation in the seminar was not restricted to friars. The resulting volume, like the seminar, is not necessarily for people who are formally "Franciscan," nor was it restricted to a scholarly audience but rather is intended for anyone who is interested in deepening a Gospel commitment in an urban context. Our goal is not only to inform but also to offer our readers the opportunity to reflectively consider conditions and possibilities for themselves. We have included some points for discussion concerning relevant elements of Franciscan tradition and Franciscan spirituality as they have developed in regard to urban life over the centuries. In addition, we challenge the reader to engage with a few current realities in urban settings.

How To Use This Book

Each article can be read on its own as a stand-alone piece, or the entire book can be read as a whole to develop a more complete understanding of the complexity of the issues. To facilitate a practical application of the material we have provided a series of reflective questions at the end of each article. We offer them not simply to broaden and deepen an intellectual understanding of the topic but rather to enable readers to engage their personal experience on the issue at hand and consider the potential for personal and communal responses. The book was written primarily for use with a group; possibilities include a group selected from within a particular ministerial setting, a reading group, a Secular Franciscan formation activity, or a group involved in staff development.

At the conclusion of the book we provide a series of integrative questions for reflection that consider convergence points or themes that cut across several articles. We offer them to allow readers another opportunity for further integration and application of the content of the book to their own lives and ministerial situations.

Ken Himes, O.F.M.
Washington Theological Union

Franciscan Life and Urban Life: A Tense Relationship

Dominic V. Monti, O.F.M.

One of my favorite scenes in Giotto's marvelous fresco cycle that covers the walls of the upper basilica of San Francesco in Assisi depicts the saint driving a horde of demons from a walled medieval town. Here the artist dramatically captures a visit Francis made to Arezzo at a time when that city was torn by civil war. From the place where he had been given hospitality on the outskirts of the town near the old cathedral he saw the demons swarming over the city, rejoicing as they incited the citizens to mutual hatred and slaughter. And so, immersing himself in prayer, Francis sent Brother Sylvester to cast out the evil spirits from the place; afterwards, the populace calmed down and the citizens reformed their civil statutes to insure justice for all, thereby undercutting the causes of division. Thus "the wisdom of a poor man entered in, brought back peace, and saved the city."[1]

Today, visitors to the basilica of St. Francis may naturally be drawn to the familiar scenes of Francis preaching to the birds or kneeling before the crib at Greccio. But the vivid depiction of his exorcising the demons reminds us of the tremendous impact the new Franciscan movement had on the cities of medieval Europe. This fresco does not simply depict an isolated incident in the life of Francis but captures an essential element of the vocation of his "Lesser Brothers": they saw themselves as heralds of the Gospel, sent to cast out the demons of greed and violence that characterized the life of medieval cities.[2]

We are well aware that Francis was frequently drawn to his beloved mountain hermitages to seek union with God, but his love for God's people also thrust him into crowded urban marketplaces to preach a message of conversion. As the thirteenth century progressed, his brothers increasingly

---

[1]As with all the scenes in this fresco cycle, Giotto based his depiction on an incident in Bonaventure's "Major Legend of St. Francis" [*Legenda major*, 6.9]. For an English translation, see *Francis of Assisi: Early Documents*, Vol. 2: *The Founder*, ed. Regis Armstrong, Wayne Hellmann, and William Short (Hyde Park, NY: New City Press, 2000), 574-75.

[2]In this paper, I am limiting my treatment to the First Order of the Franciscan family.

favored towns as the site of their communal life and ministry. A familiar medieval ditty captured this urban orientation of the friars:

> *Bernardus valles, montes Benedictus amabat*
> *Oppida Franciscus, celebres Dominicus urbes.*

> Bernard liked the valleys, Benedict the hills
> Francis the towns, Dominic the cities of renown.[3]

What the friars' medieval contemporaries observed has more and more come to the attention of modern scholars. Ever since the publication of a seminal article by Jacques LeGoff three decades ago, historians have highlighted the tendency of the new mendicant orders to locate in the expanding cities of Western Europe,[4] and the critical role they came to play in the lives of their inhabitants.[5] The noted medievalist Richard Southern has gone so far as to state: "Wherever there was a town there were friars; and without a town there were no friars."[6] The growing lure to the cities felt by the young

---

[3]Cited in William A. Hinnebusch, *The History of the Dominican Order: Origins and Growth to 1500*, vol. 1 (New York: Alba House, 1965), 260. Although this refrain notes the fact that both of the leading mendicant orders, in contrast to the monastic ones, favored urban sites, it also attests to the Dominicans' tendency to concentrate in large communities in the major cities, whereas Franciscans formed more numerous and smaller communities. See C. H. Lawrence, *The Friars: The Impact of the Mendicant Movement on Western Society* (London: Longman, 1994), 103-04.

[4]"Apostolat mendiant et fait urban dans la France médiévale: l'implantation des ordres mendiant," *Annales* 23 (1968): 335-52. Since, there have been a number of detailed studies on individual European countries. Le Goff followed up his groundbreaking work on France in "Ordres mendiant et unbanisation dans la France médievale. Etat de l'enquete," *Annales* 25 (1970): 924-46. Studies on Italy have been the most numerous; basic is Luigi Pellegrini, *Insediamenti francescani nell'Italia del duecento* (Rome: *Laurentianum*, 1984), but there are many detailed studies on individual cities. A significant study of the latter type is Daniel Lesnick, *Preaching in Medieval Florence: The Social World of Franciscan and Dominican Spirituality* (Athens, GA: University of Georgia Press, 1989). On the friars in Germany, see J. B. Freed, *The Friars and German Society in the Thirteenth Century* (Cambridge, MA: Medieval Academy of America, 1977). On England, see Janet Burton, *Monastic and Religious Orders in Britain 1000-1300* (Cambridge: Cambridge University Press, 1994).

[5]For a good brief synthesis, see Lawrence's chapter "Mission to the Towns" (102-26). The seminal study in English was Lester K. Little, *Religious Poverty and the Profit Economy in Medieval Europe* (Ithaca, NY: Cornell University Press, 1978). It is Little's thesis that "the unique achievement of the friars was their creation of new forms of religious expression specifically for the urban sector of society and the people dominant in it" (173).

[6]R. W. Southern, *Western Society and the Church in the Middle Ages* (London: Penguin Books, 1970), 286. The second half of the statement is somewhat exaggerated. Cf. Robert Brentano, "Early Franciscans and Italian Towns, " *Monks, Nuns, and Friars in Medieval Society*, ed. Edward King *et. al.*, Sewanee Medieval Studies, 4 (1989): 29-50.

Franciscan Order may well be illustrated by its first mission to England in 1224. Within six weeks of their landing in Dover the little band of twelve friars had split up into three groups, quickly heading for Canterbury, London, and Oxford – the ecclesiastical, commercial, and academic centers of the country.[7] One recent study suggests that "the friars were in many ways responsible for the most distinctively and uniquely *urban* contribution made by the church in the long history of Christianity."[8]

Such studies pose obvious questions. What accounts for this mutual attraction between friars and towns? What was the "distinctive contribution" the friars made to urban ministry that accounted for their popularity? As Franciscans perhaps we need to probe more deeply than just the question of ministry. After all, this attraction to the cities was characteristic of the mendicant orders in general. Perhaps we should sharpen our focus and ask another question: was not in fact the distinctive charism of the Friars Minor profoundly shaped by the urban reality? In other words, is there some kind of intrinsic relationship between Franciscan life and urban life? And if so, is there a creative tension in this relationship that must be maintained if Franciscan urban ministry is to be successful? These are the questions I would like to examine briefly here.[9]

The Urban Environment

One of the most striking features of Europe in the central Middle Ages (1050-1300) was the revival of urban life. For the first time since the decline

---

[7]Thomas of Eccleston, "The Coming of the Friars Minor to England," trans. Placid Hermann, in *XIIIth Century Chronicles* (Chicago: Franciscan Herald Press, 1961), 93-101.

[8]Burton, 130. This thesis has been developed most thoroughly in the work of Lester Little cited above.

[9]This essay is indebted to the criticism offered by Michael Cusato to an earlier article of mine on this topic, "'What is Ours to Do?' The Roots of Franciscan Ministry," *Friar Lines* 2.3 (Spring, 1990): 1-20, *passim*. Cf. Michael Cusato, "Hermitage or Marketplace? The Search for an Authentic Franciscan Locus in the World," in *Franciscan Leadership in Ministry*, in *Spirit and Life, A Journal of Contemporary Franciscanism*, 7 (St. Bonaventure, NY: Franciscan Institute Press, 1997), 125-148. I must admit that in retrospect, this earlier effort was perhaps not sufficiently nuanced, but it was composed for an in-house publication at a time when my province was withdrawing from a number of suburban and rural parishes in order to open a number of new urban ministries. It was in some ways intended as a support for this decision. I believed at the time, and still do, that these locales generally offer a more creative locus for contemporary Franciscan pastoral ministry, offering opportunities for work with those populations "on the margins" of society and the institutional church. Even then, however, I believe I agreed with Cusato's contention that a contemporary "re-founding" of Franciscan life today cannot be based on ministry alone: that it must include what we *are*, as well as what we *do*.

of the Roman Empire, there was a large-scale movement of people to cities. This sudden development was due not only to greater political stability, which allowed for a rebirth of long-distance trade, but also to significant developments in agriculture, which furnished a better food supply and a surplus rural population. These medieval cities were considerably smaller than their modern counterparts: by 1300 there were probably not more than sixty towns in Western Europe which had over 10,000 inhabitants, and only about a half-dozen with more than 50,000. And yet these small cities presented a threatening environment to medieval men and women, for the contrast between town and country life was much greater then than in most of our contemporary societies. Town walls marked a real frontier between two separate worlds.[10]

Home for the inhabitants of a typical farming village was a tightly knit community of perhaps 25 or 30 households. The rhythms of life, defined by immemorial custom and marked by familiar rituals, were extremely constricting but at the same time provided a deep sense of belonging. When country people moved into a town this secure sense of the world was shattered: they may have experienced greater opportunities, but they also felt a deep sense of isolation.[11] This was not simply due to the risk of anonymity in a larger setting. In the village, virtually everyone – except for the lord of the manor – was at the same subsistence level; a system of cooperative labor meant everyone rose and fell together in times of plenty or famine. In contrast, the *laissez-faire* dynamics of the new profit economy led to unbridled competition, pitting one person against another. To protect their mutual interests, workers in the same trade began to band together in guilds. But even so, sharp gulfs in income emerged. The merchants, bankers, and professionals who dominated the urban economy could amass considerable wealth, whereas the typical day laborer in the cloth industry might work

---

[10]For an excellent basic introduction to the issues in this section, especially economic expansion and the growth of cities, see *The Cambridge Illustrated History of the Middle Ages, Vol. 2: 950-1250*, ed. Robert Fossier (Cambridge Cambridge University Press, 1997), 243-395. The figures on population size are taken from page 363. See also Little on the urban background, 3-57.

[11]The sociologist Louis Wirth, in a classic article, emphasized that urban life is characterized by "the coincidence of close physical contact and distant social relations. See "Urbanism as a Way of Life," *American Journal of Sociology* 44 (1938):1. I discovered this reference in Giles Constable, *The Reformation of the Twelfth Century* (Cambridge: Cambridge University Press, 1996), 320. Constable offers a number of provocative insights on the relation of the growth of cities with religious reform.

sixteen hours a day amid horrible conditions. Surviving thirteenth-century tax records clearly indicate this class polarization; one from Orvieto may be cited as typical. The poorest people, indigents relying on alms, accounted for about 10% of the population. Another considerable segment, about 20%, owned no property, living from day to day on what they earned through their labor. The incapacitation or death of the family wage earner could quickly push such people into the ranks of the beggars.[12]

These isolating tendencies were reflected on the political level. Village life was bound by the tight strictures of manorial law. City life offered enterprising peasants freedom, but they found that it came at the price of chronic violence. Civil strife was especially endemic in northern and central Italy, where a three-sided political struggle had created a virtual power vacuum. This region was theoretically subject to the Holy Roman Emperor, who exercised authority through his feudal vassals. In the towns, these had traditionally been the local bishops, who had over the centuries absorbed the role of chief civic authority. But as the Gregorian reform agenda took hold in the twelfth century, bishops became increasingly insistent on the "liberties of the church," allying themselves with the Papacy over against the imperial prerogatives. Furthermore, the emerging commoners began to seize *de facto* power, forming sworn mutual aid societies (*compagne*) to keep peace and administer justice. Although the Emperor Frederick I Barbarossa attempted to reassert his authority, the stiff resistance he met from city dwellers forced him in 1183 to concede to them the right to form autonomous communal governments. These quickly fell under the control of the economically dominant merchants and bankers. But the struggle was not over. As time went on, the so-called lesser guilds of artisans and shopkeepers also began agitating for a voice. Meanwhile, the local bishops, with the support of the Papacy, were trying to assert their traditional rights. Communal governments were sharply divided by pro-imperial and pro-Papal factions. The situation was aggravated by the fact that local governmental structures were still in their infancy, providing neither comprehensive legislation nor an

---

[12]See Michel Mollat, *The Poor in the Middle Ages*, trans. Arthur Goldhammer (New Haven: Yale University Press, 1986), 174-77. This study offers a corrective to the overly-sanguine view of Lesnick: "the demand for labor was so great . . . that it is hard to envision a mass of chronically unemployed and starving poor . . . [in central Italy] during the thirteenth century" (23). Certainly medieval Italy did not have the huge shanty-towns surrounding cities in "Third World" countries today, but Mollat convincingly shows (115-90) that urban poverty was most certainly a problem in thirteenth century Italy.

effective administration. Families and associations of private citizens still trusted in self-help, both for mediating disputes and protecting themselves against enemies. Vendettas, even civil wars, were common.[13]

Thus urban economics and politics, characterized by greed and the quest for power, tended to isolate individuals from one another. To achieve anything, people found they had to join with others in organized groups, such as the trade guilds and the private 'mutual defense' associations. The converse was also true: a person became "an outcast . . . if he was not perceived as belonging to a group, as being isolated, vulnerable."[14] But urban communities were not a given; they had to be created by individual commitment. Such a "self-consciousness awareness of the role of the individual" tended to create in people "an oppressive sense of responsibility in isolation."[15] In this new situation which demanded personal decision making, people naturally turned to their religious faith for guidance, but found there little to assist them. The merely ritual reassurances offered by the traditional liturgy were no longer adequate. And people did not possess personal religious resources, for the vast majority of them had never received any formal instruction in their Catholic faith. This created in medieval town-dwellers an immense religious hunger. They were searching for a "word from God" to nourish them. The new social and economic realities impelled them to search for a more adequate doctrinal and ethical framework.[16]

This new situation posed severe challenges for the church, for its existing ministerial structures were ill equipped to address it. The typical priest was theologically uneducated, a situation perhaps excusable in a rural setting where his role was mainly to enact the church's rituals and transmit its oral tradition. But such a clergyman was in no position to preach effectively or offer the type of moral guidance people were demanding in the towns. And the centers of spiritual vitality – the monasteries – were by definition withdrawn from the flux of urban life. Furthermore, as the new popular classes struggled to gain power from the aristocracy, they viewed the institutional

---

[13]See especially J. K. Hyde, *Society and Politics in Medieval Italy: The Evolution of Civic Life 1000-1350* (London: St. Martin's Press, 1973), and Giovanni Tabacco, *The Struggle for Power in Medieval Italy* (Cambridge: Cambridge University Press, 1989), 182-236.

[14]Fossier, 390-91.

[15]Erik Erickson, "Ontogeny of Ritualization in Man," a 1966 article cited in Constable, 319-20.

[16]See the classic work of M.D. Chenu, *Nature, Man and Society in the Twelfth Century* (Chicago: University of Chicago Press, 1968), 202-69.

church as a political adversary, for it was an integral part of the old feudal order. Both diocesan clergy and monasteries were supported through their landed estates and obligatory tithes, setting them up as "lords" in the eyes of commoners. Confronted with the wealth and careerism of a largely inadequate clerical establishment, many lay people increasingly took the matter of religious guidance into their own hands. Townspeople who were used to banding together in trade guilds and mutual protection associations began forming religious confraternities as well. Some of these began to reflect together on the meaning of Scripture and even to preach publicly, raising the threat of heresy.[17]

We have to keep this social context in the front of our minds if we are to understand the origins of the Franciscan movement. The Friars Minor were not founded simply to "minister to" people in this urban environment. Their whole way of life, their very identity as "Lesser Brothers," was a product of it. So we must ask: what exactly did "Franciscan life" – or what Francis called "a life according to the Gospels" – originally imply when juxtaposed with the reality of "urban life"? We will see that the first Franciscans were both *reacting against* the medieval city while at the same time *responding to* its needs.

Penitents from Assisi

Assisi, the birthplace of the Franciscan movement, was a microcosm of the trends that we have just examined. Situated on the major trade route through the Italian peninsula, it was ideally situated to take advantage of the expanding economy. The town's prosperity is indicated by the fact that it was forced to expand its walls three times in a space of fifty years to accommodate its growing population.[18]

For generations, Assisi had been controlled by about twenty families of the old, landed aristocracy (*maiores*), who traditionally supported the Emperors in their perennial conflicts with the Popes. Frederick Barbarossa had rewarded their loyalty in 1160, granting Assisi the rank of an autonomous

---

[17]*Ibid.* See also R. I. Moore, *The Origins of European Dissent*, 2nd ed. (Oxford: Basil Blackwell, 1985).

[18]The best treatment in English of Assisi's history and sociology is Arnaldo Fortini, *Francis of Assisi*, trans. Helen Moak (New York, The Crossroads Publishing Co., 1981). David Flood, *Francis of Assisi and the Franciscan Movement* (Quezon City, Philippines: FIA Contact Publications, 1989), also offers a compelling portrait of Assisi society which has influenced me greatly.

county. But as the Empire and the Papacy continued to be at loggerheads in the later thirteenth century, the commoners (*minores*) of Assisi took advantage of the unstable situation. Bolting the imperial camp in 1174, they established an independent communal government. However, the upstart city was quickly overcome; in 1177 the Emperor's local representative, Conrad of Urslingen, re-feudalized Assisi, governing it from the Rocca Maggiore that dominated the town.

This was the situation into which Francis was born in 1181/82, the son of one of the town's more prosperous merchants. As a youth, he undoubtedly took part in the great revolt of 1198, when the commoners destroyed the feudal strongholds such as the hated Rocca and the town houses of the local aristocracy, many of whom took refuge in Assisi's bitter rival city, Perugia.[19] Francis continued to engage in this class struggle, fighting in the communal army, which was defeated by Perugia in 1202. The popular party in Assisi was thus forced to allow the aristocrats to return. An uneasy truce between the parties continued until 1210, when the nobility and the leading *minores* put aside their differences, entering a "Great Pact" to assure the peace and prosperity of the city. Although a communal government was again established, it was controlled by the wealthier commoners, as only they could afford the payment required for exemption from feudal levies and the right to participate as full voting citizens. By the 1220's, this latter group comprised only about a hundred families. Most of Assisi's people still were without political power.

This description of Francis's hometown has been provided, not as an *excursus* in medieval history, but as an essential element in trying to capture the genius of his movement. Too often we are tempted to read the early Franciscan sources as purely spiritual documents, without any reference to the political and economic choices made by Francis and his early brotherhood. Their conversion was not simply "religious." It involved a definite reaction against "urban life," at least as the elite who controlled Assisi defined it.

When he looked back at his life, Francis came to see the years when he shared the values and aspirations of Assisi's aspiring middle class — money and power — as a time when he "was in sin." His conversion process or "life

---

[19]On exiles and their role in Italian political life, see Randolph Starn, *Contrary Commonwealth: The Themes of Exile in Medieval and Renaissance Italy* (Berkeley: University of California Press, 1982).

Choices Made by Francis
① Spiritual
② Political
③ Economic

of penance" began around 1204 when he was "led among the lepers," accepting and serving a group of persons which had been marginalized by the city.[20] When in 1206 his growing desire "to rebuild God's house" by sharing his wealth led his father to accuse him of squandering the family assets, Francis responded by renouncing his property, family, and social status. In a sense, he chose to be a leper, literally "leaving the world" for the margins of Assisi society. There, as a hermit, he devoted himself to a life of prayer and work with the poor.[21] Two years later, Francis's life took a new turn when "the Lord gave him brothers," and "revealed to him" that they "should live according to the form of the Holy Gospel."[22]

It is important to recognize from the start that Francis believed his Gospel way of life demanded that he and his brothers maintain the social location of hermits. Therefore, they chose to dwell physically apart "from the world," in remote, abandoned places on the edges of settled Assisi, using properties which legally belonged to others. They remained outsiders to the city, living "among people considered of little worth and looked down upon, among the poor and powerless, the sick and the lepers, and the beggars by the wayside."[23] It was from the perspective of these marginalized people that they viewed the urban life of Assisi. They "left the world" in this way because they had come to see that the values of the reign of God were in sharp contrast to those that dominated the city. Instead of accepting the society driven by the lust for power and wealth in which they had been born and bred, Francis and his brothers chose "to follow the humility and poverty of

---

[20]In this and the following paragraphs I am illustrating Francis's life with quotations taken from his own *Testament*. For the complete text, see *Francis of Assisi: Early Documents* [hereafter *FA: ED*], ed. Regis Armstrong, Wayne Hellmann, and William Short, Vol. 1: *The Saint* (New York: New City Press, 1999), 124-27. On the increasing marginalization of lepers at the time, making them "the living dead," see R. I. Moore, *The Formation of a Persecuting Society* (Oxford: Basil Blackwell, 1987), 45-60.

[21]On the ambiguous canonical status of medieval hermits, see Constable, 60-65. Although hermits lived either by themselves or in small groups apart from society, their life afforded a great deal of independence, since it had no formal structures. Wandering hermits were a problem for church leaders throughout the medieval period. For more background, and the enduring eremetical element of Francis' life, see *Franciscan Solitude*, ed. A. Cirino, O.F.M. and J. Raischl (St. Bonaventure, NY: Franciscan Institute Press, 1995).

[22]*Testament* 14. In this paragraph I have followed the suggestion of David Flood, who distinguishes these three stages of Francis' conversion process recounted in the *Testament* (115, 145). This work has greatly influenced my reading of the social and economic dimensions of Francis's conversion process. However, I believe that this very emphasis in Flood's interpretation leads him to keep Francis and his brothers bound to the economy of Assisi itself, minimizing the missionary thrust of their life into new environments.

[23]*Earlier Rule*, 9.2.

our Lord Jesus Christ."[24] This was the only way they felt they could escape the vicious circle in which their contemporaries were caught and which prevented them from opening their hearts to God and each other.

And yet Francis also believed this new Gospel life involved a mission to the city. He and his brothers no longer remained simply as hermits "on the margins," because they also chose to interact on a regular basis with the other people of Assisi. David Flood expresses this paradox well: "They had left the world to get closer to people." They "re-entered the world in a new guise,"[25] changing the way they lived in it, working among other people, but using the good things of God's creation in such a way as not to deprive others of them. Although they dwelt at the Portiuncola, down in the valley some distance from Assisi, they would go back up into the city or to the leper hospices to work. There they practiced the trades they knew, but no longer for profit. Refusing to accept money as wages, they received only their necessities – food, clothing, and shelter – which they shared among themselves and with the poor. In this way, with no property to defend and no agenda of material gain, they were free to approach all people as equal in God's sight, worthy of attention and concern.

It was out of this paradoxical situation, working in the midst of a world whose values they rejected, that the early brothers began to preach a message to others: "Do penance, performing worthy fruits of penance because we shall soon die. Give and it will be given to you. Forgive and you shall be forgiven."[26] The brothers urged those who had more than they did to free themselves from "worldly concerns," to live simply, and to demonstrate the sincerity of their love for God by reconciling themselves to their enemies and by reaching out to help their less fortunate neighbors. Through the example of their own converted life and their preaching they could help their sisters and brothers who remained in the city to reject its demons of violence and greed.

Such was the primitive dialectic of Franciscan life and urban life. Perhaps now we are in a better position to understand the symbolism of the Giotto fresco, where Francis is depicted kneeling outside the walls of

---

[24]*Earlier Rule* 9.1.

[25]Flood, 16, 145.

[26]*Earlier Rule*, 21.3-5. For a good brief description of this earlier type of Franciscan penitential preaching, see Servus Gieben, "Preaching in the Franciscan Order: Thirteenth Century," in *Monks, Nuns, and Friars*, 1-9.

Arezzo. It is only because he and his brothers speak from the position of social "outsiders" that they have the power to cast out the demons that infect the life of the city.

Town-Dwellers

Within only a few years, however, this relationship of the early Franciscan movement to the city underwent a dramatic change. In just twenty-five years, between 1220 and 1245, a series of interrelated developments profoundly transformed Francis's brotherhood, forever altering its character.[27] The most obvious of these was the fraternity's explosive growth. The original brotherhood of 1209 numbered twelve men; by 1221 there were 3,000. Also, they were no longer confined to central Italy; Francis's zeal for mission had send them into the other countries of Western Europe and even to the Crusader States. More and more friars, especially those who joined the brotherhood in areas far removed from Assisi and its social dynamics, had no experience of the formative early years. Furthermore, the new recruits increasingly had different backgrounds than Francis and his first companions. More ordained clerics were entering what had been predominately a lay movement; impressed by the apostolic way of the life of the "Lesser Brothers," they viewed the new order as an ideal means for achieving a much-needed renewal of the church's preaching mission.[28]

Church leadership was beginning to respond to the changing religious situation. Led by Pope Innocent III, the Fourth Lateran Council of 1215 gave impetus to a virtual "pastoral revolution," its legislation embodying a clear program whose goal was an informed and converted laity instructed by a reformed and educated clergy.[29] While the Council mobilized an inquisito-

---

[27]The standard treatment in English of this critical era is John Moorman, *A History of the Franciscan Order from its Origins to the Year 1517* (Oxford: Clarendon Press, 1968), 46-122. However, recent research, much of it Italian, has supplanted some of Moorman's interpretations. For a good synthesis of some of this literature see the essays in *Francesco d'Assisi e il primo secolo di storia francescana*, ed. A. Bartoli Langeli and E. Prinzivalli (Turin: Biblioteca Einaudi, 1997) [hereafter cited as *Francesco*]. Especially valuable for this period are the contributions of Grado Giovanni Merlo, "Storia di frate Francesco e dell'Ordine dei Minori" (3-32), and Luigi Pellegrini, "I quadri e i tempi dell'expansione dell'Ordine" (165-201).

[28]Their perspective is captured by an outsider, the church reformer Jacques de Vitry, who was extremely enthused by the Franciscans he met in 1216: "I believe that the Lord desires to save many souls before the end of the world through such simple and poor men in order to put to shame our prelates, who are like dumb dogs unable to bark." *Letter* 1, *FA: ED* 1: 579-80.

[29]Colin Morris, *The Papal Monarchy: The Western Church from 1050 to 1250* (Oxford: Clarendon Press, 1989), 489-504. Fossier views this development as an "offensive" on the part of

16   Dominic Monti

rial process to stamp out heretical movements by force, it also recognized that strenuous efforts would have to be made to provide a trained clergy who could bring the laity to a reasonable understanding of the essentials of Christian belief and practice. The chief vehicles of this ministry – aimed at a still largely illiterate population – would be through doctrinal preaching of "faith and morals" and one-to-one pastoral guidance in the sacrament of penance. Popes Honorius III (1216-27) and especially his successor, Gregory IX (1227-41), increasingly came to view the Friars Minor as the "suitable men, powerful in word and work," envisioned by the Council decrees to exercise this pastoral mission.[30] By 1237 Gregory could state that the purpose of the Franciscan Order was to provide co-workers of the bishops, specifically through their preaching against heresy and hearing the confessions of the faithful.[31] Thus, from both within and without, the Order was rapidly being propelled in a new direction.

Such a focused mission also involved a shift in social location for the Lesser Brothers. No longer were they *working among* other townspeople at manual and service trades, speaking a word of good news or challenge, but *ministering to* them as pastoral agents of the church. This change transformed all the friars' relationships with the city. First of all, it demanded new living arrangements. The pattern common in the early days, where the friars dwelt on the outer fringes of the town, entering it only to work and preach, could no longer be sustained. Pressures from their audience and their own desire to engage in ministry led the friars to seek permanent dwellings within the town. This trend was already evident in Northern Europe as early as the mid 1220's; the friars' increasing focus on pastoral ministry made them urban residents there almost from the start. And in Italy, their original homeland, they soon began abandoning the primitive hermitages. For example, in 1236, only ten years after Francis' death, the Archbishop of Ravenna addressed a letter to the clergy of Bologna, seeking their help in the construction of a Franciscan convent within that city, explaining the need for this as follows:

Purpose of Franciscans

church leaders to have official teachings take effect in all facets of the life of Christendom (424-27).

[30]A phrase from canon 10 of Lateran IV, which had mandated that bishops appoint suitable men to assist them in the ministry of preaching and hearing confessions. The basic study of this development, see Lawrence Landini, *The Causes of the Clericalization of the Order of Friars Minor* (Chicago: Franciscan Herald Press, 1968).

[31]*FA: ED*, 1: 575-76.

The house of the Friars Minor of Bologna at Santa Maria de Puliola is so distant from the city that clerics and students are unable to reach it at appropriate times for lectures and sermons. Furthermore, the general population of the city cannot easily reach it to make their confessions and to hear the word of God and other things that pertain to the salvation of their souls.[32]

Such a move was not simply physical. As the friars became more and more focused on providing this pastoral ministry, they were quickly becoming urban "insiders," participating in medieval urban life much like everyone else. The friars were offering a valuable service that other people wanted. But providing such a service brought tremendous consequences. First of all, it demanded that they have their own churches. It also required that they have larger dwellings, which could provide within crowded cities the quiet space formerly afforded them by their hermitages. Their ministry brought them into fierce competition with the diocesan clergy, which led to a torrent of Papal privileges defending their rights. And it demanded new means of economic support. Friars engaged in full-time ministry no longer could spend time working with their hands in order to earn their keep; the spiritual commodities they were providing were much too valuable. Instead, these preachers and confessors had to depend on the free-will offerings of their audience.

Most friars soon accepted all these changes as natural. By the third quarter of the century, an anonymous Franciscan could offer three arguments why the brothers dwelt in cities: an apostolic one, that the pastoral mission of the order was best fulfilled in the urban context; an economic one, that mendicant poverty depended on the support of a sizeable population; and a practical one, that the countryside was too insecure a place for an order without landed estates to establish a stable religious life.[33] Each of

---

[32]*Acta franciscana e tabulariis Bononiensis deprompta* I, ed. Bonaventura Giordani, *Analecta Franciscana* 9 (1927): 4. A fine recent scholarly summary of the move of the friars into the towns and their ministry as town-dwellers is Antonio Rigon, "Frati minori e societa locali," in *Francesco*, 259-81.

[33]In the work, "Determinations of Questions on the Rule of the Friars Minor," included among the works of Bonaventure *Opera omnia* (Quaracchi), 8:340-41; scholars today tend to view it as inauthentic. There is no doubt however, that it comes from the later thirteenth century. See Pellegrini, 123-53; Ignatius Brady, "The Writings of St. Bonaventure Concerning the Franciscan Order, " *Miscellanea Francescana* 75 (1975): 89-112.

these reasons presupposes a very different reality from the primitive life of the first brothers; it takes for granted a certain symbiosis of Franciscan life and urban life.

This second phase of Franciscan life has sometimes been criticized as a "betrayal" of Francis's "life according to the Gospel."[34] Others have seen in the middle decades of the thirteenth century (1230-1270) a real flowering and maturation of Francis's original charism, albeit in quite different dress. One of these is Heribert Roggen, who more thirty years ago argued that the dialectical relationship of Franciscan life and urban life in the thirteenth century led to a dynamic synthesis.[35] One the one hand, he saw the Franciscan movement as a creative expression of the values and aspirations that characterized urban life over against those of traditional feudalism. On the other hand, Roggen recognized that Franciscans also profoundly challenged many negative dimensions of that same urban culture. Thus the characteristic Franciscan values – brotherhood, poverty, and freedom – represent a synthesis: they are an expression of the best elements of medieval urban life and a rejection of the worst. In other words, the friars owed much of their appeal to the fact that they were modeling to their contemporaries the way converted urban Christians should live.

Franciscans continued to see themselves as preaching by "example" as well as by "word." Most recent studies of the mendicant impact on the urban life of medieval Europe focus on what the friars **did**.[36] Roggen reminds us that a large measure of their success was due to what they **were**. First of all, the very notion of "being a brother" expressed the deepest social aspirations of the commoners of the medieval town. A brotherhood was not a hierarchical order; it existed in the concrete, created out of the reciprocal relationship of each brother – or sister – to the other; each had a vital and constituent part to play. The Lesser Brothers, unlike traditional monastic communities, paid no heed to their recruits' family backgrounds. Titles of rank ('abbot' and 'prior') were banned. And unlike the diocesan clergy, advancement did not depend on one's social connections. The Order was a "meritocracy": if

---

[34]Prominent among these critics is David Flood, who devotes a chapter to "the movement waylaid" (148-67).

[35]H. Roggen, *Die Lebensform des heiligen Franziskus von Assisi in ihrem Verhaltnis zur feudalen und burgerlichen Gesellschaft Italiens* (Mechelen: St. Franciscus Uitgeverij, 1965). I owe my appreciation of this work to the perceptive comments of John V. Fleming, *An Introduction to the Franciscan Literature of the Middle Ages* (Chicago: Franciscan Herald Press, 1977), 16-19.

[36]The studies of Lawrence and Lesnick cited above are good examples.

talented, a friar could be sent on for the best educational opportunities available; if he showed leadership potential, his peers could elect him as a local or regional superior. Yet despite this ability to "better oneself," so basic to the self-identity of the urban population, Franciscans still remained *lesser* brothers. Unlike other clergy, they never obtained a landed benefice, nor were they supported by tithes. They held a position of authority only at the sufferance of their brothers; their term of service ended, they returned to the ranks. So townspeople could identify with these brothers who were on the same level as themselves, people "working for a living." But at the same time, the newly urbanized Franciscans' commitment to be men of penance still made them reject two of the characteristic goals of the upwardly mobile middle classes – real estate and money, which offered the temptation of entering into the profit economy. Ownership of the brothers' houses had to remain in the hands of others, and they lived from day to day by the fruit of their labor, accepting alms in kind – not money that could be accumulated – in return for their spiritual services.

Thus the case can be made that despite their change of social location, these second and third generation Franciscans still were maintaining some very real elements of their original life as "outsiders." It was out of this context – identification with, yet challenge to, the values of the urban population – that the friars creatively developed a pastoral ministerial strategy responding to their needs. From their stance as converted men, they could move out to bring a message of 'penance' to their hearers, calling them to recognize and confront the demonic forces which all too often dominated their lives. The chief means by which the friars in thirteenth century Europe accomplished this were: 1) preaching both to the general population and to specific groups within society, trying to reach the widest possible audience, proclaiming the demands of the Gospel and calling all people to conversion; 2) hearing confessions and providing spiritual direction, thus assisting individuals who had responded to their message and desired to turn more deeply to God's call and implement Gospel values in their daily lives; 3) supporting confraternities and other forms of associations for laypeople who wished to support each other in their life of conversion and join together in practical ways to express their love of God and neighbor.

In order to provide some understanding of the connection of the friars' ministries with urban life, let us turn briefly to the first of these. Preaching occupied pride of place among Franciscan ministries, for it yielded the converted men and women essential to other forms of ministry.[37] The thirteenth century chronicler Salimbene describes many of his friar contemporaries who were noted for their success as preachers. They all shared two basic abilities: they could make an audience comprehend and remember their message, and they could motivate those who heard it to change their lives.[38] Both built on natural talent, but they were also acquired skills. To help their brothers develop them, Franciscans were among the major contributors to a new genre of literature, the preaching manual (*artes praedicandi*). These handbooks had as their goal the traditional objectives of classical rhetoric: to teach, to delight, and to persuade.[39] But they emphasized that the preacher would best achieve these ends by following a highly sophisticated art.

The first objective, teaching an audience what they should believe and how they should act, was accomplished by the logical and thorough development of a topic. Typically such a handbook first instructed the preacher how to select an appropriate theme, announced through a brief Scriptural verse. It then explained how to develop the body of the sermon in a logical fashion, typically by a process of dividing and subdividing the text into distinct units, each one making a doctrinal or moral point. The validity of each point was generally proven by a combination of logical arguments, appeals to authority (Biblical texts or patristic authors), and illustrative anecdotes (*exempla*) drawn from history, nature, or everyday life. Such highly structured sermons were ideal for the purpose of urban catechesis. The technique helped the preacher clarify his own thought, sorting out the points he wanted to make. The process of logical division of the text-generally into threes-helped the audience remember them. Scholars have pointed out the correspondence between this new type of preaching and the quest for systematization and quantification that increasingly marked urban life: the

---

[37]My discussion of Franciscan preaching is based chiefly on the treatments of David d'Avray, *The Preaching of the Friars: Sermons Diffused from Paris before 1300* (Oxford: Clarendon Press, 1985), and Fleming (110-89). Gieben (1-27) offers a good brief description of the shift from the earlier penitential preaching to popular doctrinal preaching characteristic of this second generation. Although devoted to the fifteenth century, there is a fine summary of medieval Franciscan popular preaching in Franco Mormando, *The Preacher's Demons: Bernardino of Siena and the Social Underworld of Early Renaissance Italy* (Chicago: University of Chicago Press, 1999), 7-21.

[38]For example, see Salimbene's description of the German Berthold of Regensburg, in *Chronicle of Salimbene de Adam*, trans. by Joseph Baird, Giuseppe Baglivi, and John Kane (Binghamton: Medieval Renaissance Text and Studies, 1986), 566-70.

[39]As transmitted by Augustine's *De doctrina christiana* (cf. Mormando, 8).

teaching method of the schools, the organization of communal life, and the realities of the money economy.[40]

But a Franciscan preacher was not simply aiming to impart a clear, comprehensible message; his ultimate aim was to motivate his hearers to change the way they lived. Like Francis, he wanted them to "convert," to ✗"do penance." Certainly the logical arguments intrinsic to the thematic sermon were themselves persuasive to some extent, but Franciscan preachers tended to present their points in a way that appealed more to the emotions than the intellect. They would have agreed with the great American evangelical Jonathan Edwards, who argued that the seat of religion was in the affections: people are moved more by gut feelings than they are by intellectual arguments.[41] The preacher's task is to touch that deeper level within a person – the "heart" – which alone can motivate true conversion. Following the injunction of Alexander of Hales "to measure the word of God according to the capacity of their hearers,"[42] when Franciscans preached to popular audiences they tended to tone down the intellectual slant of the typical Scholastic sermon for an educated clerical gathering. Rather, they played up the vivid narratives and other word pictures that would best hit home in the hearer's own human experience. After all, the purpose of a sermon was to have its hearers confront God's call in their own lives, move them to conversion of heart (a new way of viewing their life), and so to action and involvement.[43] An eye-witness to Francis's own preaching related that he did not really "preach" in a formal sense; he "harangued" – that is, he used the language of the politician or merchant whose goal was to win people over, to sell a product.[44] Although his educated brothers did follow the technique of

---

[40]E.g., Jacques LeGoff, *Time, Work, and Culture in the Middle Ages*, trans. Arthur Goldhammer (Chicago: University of Chicago Press, 1980).

[41]Jonathan Edwards composed his treatise, *The Religious Affections* in 1746 to defend the evangelical methods of the Great Awakening; see *Works of Jonathan Edwards*, ed. John Smith, vol. 2 (New Haven: Yale University Press, 1959), 91-124. Bonaventure based himself on the primacy of the affections to explain why God's own word in Scripture takes the form it does: "This teaching exists so that we might become good and be saved, and this is not achieved through speculation alone, but by a disposition of the will . . . Now our affections are moved more strongly by examples than by arguments, by promises than by reasoning, by devotion than by definition . . . " *Breviloquium*, prol. 6.

[42]Cited by d'Avray, 186.

[43]Lesnick, 134-71, examines this in detail.

[44]Thomas, later archdeacon of Split on the Dalmatian coast, who witnessed a sermon by Francis in the market place of Bologna in 1220 (see *FA: ED*, 2: 807-08). Thomas describes Francis speaking in the style of the *contio*, disdained by professional rhetoricians. See Enrico Artifoni, "Gli uomini dell'assemblea. L'oratoria civile, i concionatori, e I predicatori nella so-

the preaching manuals in their popular sermons, they simplified its form so that their points could be readily absorbed and directed their appeal principally to people's emotions and imaginations.

This approach to preaching had an intrinsic connection to the other two principal ministries of the friars: one-to-one guidance of people in confession, and assisting groups of converted laity. Early Franciscan theologians reflected the appeal to a person's affections in their understanding of the sacrament of Penance.[45] They believed that conversion of life had to be marked both by recognition of one's sinful state and true contrition – a deep sorrow for sin that included a will to repent and lead a new life. Thus Franciscan authors argued that the ritual elements of the sacrament-confession of sin by the penitent, absolution by the priest, and performance of the assigned works of "penance" – reconciled a person only on a juridical level; they removed the penalty (*poena*) which was imposed by sin. On the other hand, guilt (*culpa*) – the state of personal alienation of the sinner from God-could be removed by only interior contrition, that movement of a person's will which springs from a motive of true love of God and determines to act justly. Men and women experienced contrition when they began to grasp the depth of God's love for them and their own failure to respond to it; such remorse would lead to a decision to change one's life. As a prominent Franciscan preacher, Bonaventure of Iseo (c. 1247) put it: "affective love" (contrition) must lead to "effective love" (making peace with God and with one's neighbor).[46] In this way, Franciscan ministry appealed to the urban value of freedom; the preacher tried to make the listeners realize that they were responsible actors in their own salvation with control over their own futures. God's love was one that enabled them to act: to get up, leave the past behind, and change their lives through an effective love of God and neighbor.

Such penitential preaching gave a tremendous impetus to the movement of converted laypersons to form "brotherhoods of penance." These groups, which often asked Franciscan friars to serve as their chaplains, expressed on

---

cieta communale," *La predicazione dei Frati della meta del '200 alla fine del '300*. Atti del XXII convegno internazionale, Societá internazionale di studi francescani (Spoleto, 1995), 141-88.

[45]This is nicely developed in David Jeffrey, *The Early English Lyric and Franciscan Spirituality* (Lincoln, NE: University of Nebraska Press, 1975), 43-82.

[46]This Bonaventure, not as well known as his namesake, Bonaventure of Bagnoregio, the Paris theologian and general minister of the Order, was very active as a popular preacher and administrator in the Order, mainly in Northern Italy, between 1238 and 1273. See Jeannette Hurst, "Franciscan Preaching, Communal Politics, and the Struggle between Papacy and Empire in Northern Italy, 1230-1268," Ph.D. dissertation, Cornell University, 1987, 48-51, 65-75.

[handwritten annotation:] Penance - reconciled others on jurridical level
Guilt - removed only by inner conversion

a religious level the characteristic awareness of medieval town-dwellers that they needed to band together to accomplish their objectives. These "brothers and sisters of penance" took practical actions of "effective love," to use Bonaventure of Iseo's phrase, to counteract the evils of urban life. They attacked the sources of violence in a practical way by refusing to carry weapons. They renounced greed by a commitment to live in a simple manner. They moved to assist the "outsiders" of urban society through works of charity, organizing and serving in hospices for the sick and the poor.[47] At times Franciscan penitential preaching had an impact on the lives of medieval cities, not simply indirectly through the witness of converted individuals, but directly, on the very structures of government. Bonaventure of Iseo, Gerard of Modena, and the celebrated Anthony of Padua were only several of a number of thirteenth-century friars who were called in by city governments to serve as advisors in the task of social reform. These friars were accepted by leaders of the commune as "outsiders" who had no vested interests to protect. Speaking from an objective perspective, the friar could suggest appropriate means for assuring more effective justice for all the citizens of the commune, thus achieving greater civic peace.[48]

Settling In? Difficulties Maintaining a Tension

Such a healthy but tension-filled dialectic of Franciscan life and urban life was difficult to maintain. As an illustration, let us look at the next phase of Franciscan history. In the last decades of the thirteenth century, the Lesser Brothers' relationship with the city entered upon yet another change. In an almost imperceptible fashion, the friars began to "settle in" as part of the local religious establishment.[49] Successful in fending off the opposition of disgruntled diocesan clergy at the Second Council of Lyons (1274) and favored with even more ministerial privileges from the Papacy, the Franciscans capitalized on their success. They embarked on massive construction

---

[47]See Moorman, 216-25. A more recent treatment, with extensive bibliography, is provided by Giovanna Casagrande, "Un Ordine per i laici: Penitenza e Penitenti nel Duecento," in *Francesco*, 237-255.

[48]This topic is well developed in the studies of J. Hurst (see note 46) and Augustine Thompson, *Revival Preaching and Politics in Thirteenth Century* (Oxford: Clarendon Press, 1992).

[49]The developments described in this and the following paragraph are treated in Moorman, 177-204, 307-368. See also Duncan Nimmo, *Reform and Division in the Medieval Franciscan Order* (Rome: Capuchin Historical Institute, 1987), 51-232.

projects, dramatically enlarging their churches to accommodate their huge audience. In Italy, Santa Croce in Florence and Santa Maria Gloriosa (the Frari) in Venice are probably the two most significant examples of this building campaign.[50] The trend towards a more comfortable style of life among the friars themselves, already lamented by earlier general ministers like John of Parma and Bonaventure, accelerated. This time few leaders protested. Local friaries began to accept legacies and donations of fields and orchards to ensure adequate upkeep of their houses and ministries. Monetary alms became more and more frequent. In 1322 Franciscans officially assumed ownership of their properties. They were now "buying into" the economy of the city.

Furthermore, fourteenth century Franciscans became more entrenched socially by the simple fact that they were all pretty much "local boys." Rather than being transferred about from place to place as they had been previously, friars now tended to enter the Franciscan community in their hometowns and remain there for the rest of their lives. In Italy, there was even a neighborhood identification, as the churches of the major mendicant orders became the unofficial gathering places for the various quarters of a city. The friars had also become more monastic. They spent most of their lives within the walls of their cloister, exercising their ministry mainly within their own church, the typical friar being given permission to go out "into town" only infrequently. The friars' churches became the burial place of choice for the social elite, and more importantly, the convents themselves were filled with the sons and brothers of the prominent families of the city. Were Franciscans still maintaining the earlier dialectic-affirming the best of urban values while rejecting their "demonic" aspect? Did this growing identification of the friars with the urban establishment bring about some subtle shifts in the message of conversion the friars preached?

There has not been as much scholarly work on the Franciscans in the later Middle Ages as in the seminal thirteenth century, but one valuable study by Bernadette Paton has examined the sermons of friars in Siena during the century 1380-1480.[51] Paton's work reveals that, especially through their preaching, the mendicant orders continued to act as the collective social conscience of the commune. But her study forces the reader to ask a

---

[50]The new Santa Croce was begun c. 1290, the Frari, c. 1330.
[51]Bernadette Paton, *Preaching Friars and the Civic Ethos: Siena, 1380-1480* (London: Centre for Medieval Studies, 1992).

probing question: did the friars' message prophetically challenge Siena's inhabitants to convert more deeply to Gospel values or simply voice the moral consensus of the city's ruling classes? Perhaps the clearest answer Paton offers – and one central to Franciscan preaching – concerns the issue of wealth and the corresponding demands of charity.[52] By the fourteenth century, it appears that the friars had muted their original message denouncing the superfluity of riches, adopting instead the Aristotelian notion of wealth as a synonym for virtuous industry. They viewed wealth as a blessing: it provided the occasion for financially successful people to exercise virtue through caring for the needy. And they tended to emphasize that alms should be distributed to the "deserving poor" – not to those whose poverty was self-induced as a result of laziness and prodigality. This "conscious or unconscious acceptance of secular attitudes to wealth" by most of the Sienese friar preachers – Dominicans, Augustinians, Conventual Franciscans – made them "fundamentally conservative in their calls for charity." Unlike their counterparts of an earlier age, there is no suggestion that governmental reform was needed to assure a more just distribution of the goods of the commune.

Paton indicates that there was only one significant exception to this pattern of virtual identification of friar values and dominant communal values – the new Observant Franciscan reform.[53] The Observant preachers, although acknowledging the social utility of wealth, tended to identify themselves with the poor of the city rather than the moneyed classes. They did so because they experienced life from the perspective of the poor. Bernardino of Siena, for example:

> emphasizes the physical realities contingent on indigency, stressing the misery, squalor, and discomfort of hunger and cold, thereby inviting his congregation to sympathize directly with the needy, and seeking to move them to charity through a sense of compassion rather than duty. He consciously aligns himself with the receivers rather than the givers, citing from his own experience of begging for bread to illustrate the difficulties and degradation inherent in

---

[52]Paton , 166-209, *passim.*

[53]On the rise of the Observant reform, its original eremetical emphasis, and its growing involvement in popular preaching, see Moorman (369-384, 441-78) and Nimmo (364-428, 576-96).

the position of those dependent on their sustenance upon citizens better-off than themselves.[54]

Bernardino and other Observant preachers sought to dissociate poverty from the stigma of idleness that society had attached to it, and to focus attention on the poor as persons having inherent dignity. This caused them to examine the causes of poverty, making their hearers aware of the fact that many times the condition of the poor was not their fault; rather, they were victims of unjust economic conditions.

This attention on the systemic causes of poverty led many Observant preachers to call not simply for more charity, but for social reform legislation. A major part of their campaign was directed against the practice of usury, the harsh interest charged by bankers on loans, that kept the poor in a cycle of poverty.[55] The Observants argued for the creation of an alternative to this oppressive financial system, a type of non-profit pawn shop called a *monte di pietà* (literally, "a heap of compassion").[56] The first *monte* of which accurate records exist was formed in Perugia in 1462. The idea appears to have been the inspiration of several local friars who suggested that their confrere, Michael of Milan, be invited to preach the public Lenten sermon series. Michael hit hard on the theme of social justice; the consequent public outcry against the usurers forced the town council to accede to the friars' idea and set up a *monte di pietà*. An initial endowment from government funds, thereafter supplemented by private donations, created a fund for lending purposes; the borrower put up a pledge in return for a cash loan. The operations of the *monte* were overseen by a board of directors composed of representatives of the commune and the church. The concept quickly spread throughout Italy, spearheaded by other Observant preachers such as Bernardino of Feltre. However, the *monti* soon aroused a storm of opposition. Obviously, the financial establishment was totally opposed to them, but the friars soon found themselves under theological attack as well. A number

---

[54]Paton, 203-204.

[55]On this campaign, and its anti-Jewish flavor, see Mormando, 164-218.

[56]For a brief treatment of the *monti di pietà*, see Moorman, 528-32. Alberto Ghinato, *Studi e Documenti intorno ai primitivi Monti di Pietà*, 5 vols. (Rome: Antonianum, 1956-63) collected much of the early documentation on the movement. A good recent study in English is Carol Bresnahan Menning, *Charity and State in Late Renaissance Italy: The Monte di Pietà of Florence* (Ithaca: Cornell University Press, 1993), with ample bibliography.

of prominent Augustinian and Dominican friars demanded that the *monti* be abolished since they were violating the church's moral teaching by charging a small interest (about 2%) to meet their expenses. One wonders if this theological attack was motivated by the connection these orders had to the local financial establishment. The lengthy debate finally ended at the Fifth Lateran Council in 1515, when Pope Leo X gave the *monti* his full approval.

But what was the reason for the Observants' social activity in the first place? What was the cause of their overt identification with the poor? The answer is not hard to find: the Observant reform had attempted to recapture some of the earlier relation of the Franciscan movement towards the city. They had first of all regained a certain "distance" from it by re-claiming a strong eremetical component in their Franciscan life, and by abandoning the corporate ownership of property, the money donations and endowments which had bound their Conventual brethren to the dominant social classes. They also had left their monastery walls to mingle with the poor and return to the old ideal of itinerant preaching. They had once again "left the world" to get closer to people.

I have ended this essay with fifteenth century Siena, not to praise the Observants or to condemn the Conventuals. Both could claim to be carrying on a Franciscan preaching tradition. But their story does force us to confront the issue of ministerial effectiveness. For the fact remains that it was the Observants who increasingly captured the attention of their contemporaries, as evidenced both in the impact of their popular preaching and their own explosive growth in membership. This example suggests that a truly effective Franciscan urban ministry emerges in good part from the way that Franciscans themselves live in the midst of the city and from the attitudes they embody towards its dominant values. The Observants in fifteenth century Siena experienced a burst of creative ministerial energy because they recaptured some of the same tension between Gospel life and urban life that had accounted for the success of the friars in thirteenth century Assisi.

This brief historical overview may thus offer some lessons for Franciscans who would engage in urban ministry today. If we are to bring an authentic Franciscan presence to the city, it cannot simply be as more effective social workers, more dynamic preachers, or more efficient pastoral leaders. Franciscan ministry must flow out of a Franciscan way of life. Francis had experienced the challenge posed by the new cities of the Middle Ages; he knew the social, political, and economic realities that governed them and

This brief historical overview may thus offer some lessons for Franciscans who would engage in urban ministry today. If we are to bring an authentic Franciscan presence to the city, it cannot simply be as more effective social workers, more dynamic preachers, or more efficient pastoral leaders. Franciscan ministry must flow out of a Franciscan way of life. Francis had experienced the challenge posed by the new cities of the Middle Ages; he knew the social, political, and economic realities that governed them and he shared the aspirations of their residents. And yet he also rejected the perversion of those values that he came to see were antithetical to the Gospel. He and his brothers modeled the way a follower of Christ could live meaningfully and fully in the city. It was because Francis stood at some distance outside Arezzo that he could gain a perspective on the true roots of the city's problems and thus speak a message of peace to its self-destructive inhabitants.

What is our contemporary Franciscan stance? Does our Franciscan way of life likewise distance us from the demonic elements of our own urban reality, thus providing us a perspective for an effective mission in it? How do we leave our world to get closer to people?

Dominic Monti, O.F.M., is a friar of the Holy Name Province. He has served as professor of Church History at Washington Theological Union. He is currently a faculty member of the Department of Theology at St. Bonaventure University, St. Bonaventure, NY.

Questions For Reflection

1. A sociologist has suggested that urban life is characterized by "the coincidence of close physical contact and distant social relations." What are the "demonic elements" of contemporary urban life?

2. In what ways do we as contemporary Franciscan men and women gain "critical distance" from our present urban societies? Do we in fact share the values of the politically and economically dominant sectors of our cities?

3. How do we "leave our world to get closer to people," especially the poor and marginalized? If we do not have this critical distance, what obstacles lie in our path?

An Invitation to the Franciscan Family

Beverly A. Carroll

Stony the road we trod,
Bitter the chastening rod,
Felt in the days when hope unborn had died;
Yet with a steady beat,
Have not our weary feet
Come to the place for which our people sighed?
We have come over a way that with tears has been
watered
We have come treading our path through the blood of the
slaughtered
Out from the gloomy past,
Till now we stand at last
Where the bright gleam of our bright star is cast." [1]

Dear Followers of St. Francis,

I begin this letter at the opening of this new millennium, a Jubilee Year of the Lord's Favor. The words in the above song, taken from the Negro National Anthem, "Lift Ev'ry Voice and Sing," resonates with the feelings of so many African American Catholics. Yet I continue to have a beautiful dream; in this dream I am accepted for who I am, the darker sister, Catholic from birth, a product of city life, and matriculated in white colleges and universities. In the dream I am respected when I speak, for "our" way of doing ministry, and for telling the "overcoming" stories handed down from generation to generation. In my dream I am selected to give the Plenary Address at Convocations and not just do a workshop. At work, I am surrounded by African Americans serving in a variety of leadership roles and am not the token Black, and the Catholic Church in America wants to minister to me. But the dream ends the same way every time: I wake up.

---

[1]"Lift Evr'y Voice and Sing," text by James Weldon Johnson; tune by J. Rosamund Johnson, in the *Lead Me Guide Me Hymnal*, 291.

What are the historical and present-day complexities of evangelizing African Americans to the Catholic Church? How do these relate to the vision and followers of St. Francis? How can we minister to this community with a renewed sense of interest and energy? This brief essay will present some thoughts based on a particular life experience, and suggest a response for future Franciscan action.

The Past

Thanks to the work of Father Cyprian Davis, O.S.B., much is now known about the early days of Africans on these shores. His research shows that the first Africans to arrive in what is now the continental United States were Spanish-speaking and Roman Catholic. The colony of St. Augustine baptismal registers from 1565 witness the presence of Blacks among the first inhabitants of St. Augustine. Only two miles north of St. Augustine the town of Santa Theresa was located, a town of freed slaves willing to receive fugitive slaves. This first all-Black settlement in the United States was a Catholic town.[2]

For decades, however, the Catholic Church was implicated in the institution of slavery. Members of religious orders as well as diocesan priests were slave owners. In general, American bishops shied away from any pronouncements on the issue of slavery. While many Protestants were divided over the question, American Catholics were never divided. Immigrant Catholics, moreover, found instant sympathy within the Democratic Party and saw unslaved African Americans as rivals in their attempts to find employment and a place in American society. But Rome took another position. Pope Gregory XVI condemned the slave trade and slavery.[3]

After the Civil War, there was still considerable racial prejudice and suspicion. The Church was slow to reach out to the newly emancipated slaves. Bishop Martin J. Spalding [1810-1872], Archbishop of Baltimore, led the U.S. Bishops in a discussion on what was referred to as "The most urgent duty of all," a discussion on the future status of the Negro. "Four million of these unfortunates are thrown on our Charity, and they silently but eloquently appeal for help. It is a golden opportunity for reaping a harvest of

---

[2]Cyprian Davis, *The History of the Black Catholics in the United States* (New York, NY: Crossroad Publishing Company, 1990), 30-33.
    [3]Davis, 39-41.

souls, which neglected may not return."[4] With the concurrence of the Holy
See, Bishop Spalding had a plan to establish a national ordinariate to coordinate the pastoral care and evangelization of the nation's 150,000 black
Catholics. It is recorded that the assembled bishops rejected the proposal,
and the "golden opportunity for a harvest of souls was lost."[5] In the end, the
bishops urged religious to come from Europe to take over the evangelization
of the Black population. On the other hand, there was a drastically different
Protestant response. Free Africans needed opportunities for self-expression,
fuller involvement in the service of the worship of God, and a center for
pooling resources. Secondly, "Black Protestant churches gave the Negro a
growing sense of dignity and self-respect with its emphasis on plain and
simple gospel which the unlearned could understand and to fill every office
in the Church for which he had the capability."[6] This form of religion gave
rise to what has become The Black Church.

Despite the lack of an organized Catholic response to or interest in the
African American community, there were dedicated religious men and
women and laity who got involved and advocated for African Americans.
African American religious women played a pivotal role in the community.
Their religious sisterhood made a unique contribution as they strove to
meet the needs of the people. Oftentimes without recognition as women
religious, the sisters took in children, educated them and taught them the
catechism.[7] It was by the grace of God that the Oblate Sisters of Providence
and the Holy Family Sisters managed to survive the dark days of slavery and
they still exist.[8] Also prominent in this effort was Mother Katherine Drexel,
a wealthy Philadelphia heiress who used her wealth to further evangelization
among Blacks and Native Americans. Mother Katherine built, and her sisters continue to run, the only African American Catholic University, Xavier,
in New Orleans, Louisiana.[9] Another heroic story is told about the Franciscan Handmaids of the Most Pure Heart of Mary who moved from Georgia
to New York in 1922. Having very little in the way of financial resources
and without any work to do in Georgia, the Handmaids left Savannah and

---

[4]Cited in "The Black Catholic Experience," in *U.S. Catholic Historian*, 5/1 (1986), 10.
[5]"The Black Catholic Experience," in *U.S. Catholic Historian*, 5/1 (1986), 10.
[6]C. Eric Lincoln and Lawrence H. Mamiya, *The Black Church in the African American Experience*, (Durham: Duke University Press, 1990) 176-78.
[7]"The Black Catholic Experience," *U.S. Catholic Historian*, 5/1 (1986), 4-5.
[8]Report of the National Black Catholic Symposium, Diocese of Detroit, 1985, 55.
[9]Davis, 254.

went to New York City. The Sisters established themselves in Harlem, operating a soup kitchen (which is still open), running a school for the children, and providing a home for the homeless.[10]

Black lay Catholics were making their presence felt in the Church at the
same time. Under the leadership of Daniel Rudd (1854-1933), founder of
the *American Catholic Tribune*, this Black Catholic weekly newspaper dealt
with issues of social justice. Rudd organized through his newspaper a Convention for Black Catholics (later to be changed to a Congress for Black
Catholics) to give their agenda some authority. The premise of these Congresses was that the Catholic Church was the single great hope for American
Blacks. An underlying goal was to bring about a massive conversion of
Blacks to Catholicism.

Five lay Black Catholic Congresses took place between 1889 and 1894.
In an age when little was written on social justice in the United States, these
Black Catholics made social justice the centerpiece of their ecclesiology.
The Congress agendas dealt with education, racial segregation in the
Church, social justice and evangelization, and discrimination. At the Black
Catholic Congress held in 1889 there was a call for admittance of Blacks to
labor unions, for an end to poor housing, for more schools, and for recogni-
tion of other social needs. The second and third Congresses likewise
stressed the importance of education, but they also discussed racial segregation in the Catholic Church. While gratitude was stressed at the fourth
Congress, there was a *proviso*: the Church's teaching on racial justice must
become the Church's practice by her members. If this were to happen, the
Congress members felt, the whole colored race would be banging down the
[the Church's] doors for admittance, anxious to be of that faith which
teaches and practices the sublime essence of human rights.[11] Many of the
demands of the Congresses were never met, but their goals gave a sense of
unity to African American Catholics.

The Black Freedom movement of the 1950s and 60s was a period of de-
cisive change in the Black Community. The Civil Rights Movement brought
an end to segregation and fostered legal equality and opportunity.[12] The
American Dream as championed by Rev. Dr. Martin Luther King Jr. and

---

[10]Davis, 240-42.
[11]"The Black Catholic Community, 1880-1987," *U.S. Catholic Historian*, 7 (1988): 158-70.
[12]Maulana Karenga, *Introduction to Black Studies*, (Los Angeles: University of Sankore
Press, 1989), 125-261.

others captured the imagination of many Christian Believers. The symbol of a land of freedom where people of all races, creeds, and nationalities could live together as beloved community was grounded in God's creation and our universal humanity.[13] Until the late 1950s the Catholic Church paid little attention to the Black Community even though it was growing steadily. The Bishops of the United States spoke out for the first time on racism in 1958 when they issued a statement condemning racial segregation.

The Civil Rights era became the impetus for many religious communities; however, to stand up for justice in the Black community. This is clearly true of the Franciscan friars. One friar tells how there was absolutely nothing for the Black people, nothing for the children to do, no support for families, and it became his primary focus to set up athletic teams for the children, do street ministry and find housing which would be rented to Blacks. Also living out the Dream were Friars in Anderson and Greenville, South Carolina, Winston-Salem, North Carolina, and Pensacola, Florida, who became beacons of hope for the people in those communities. In another part of the country, there was a very zealous scholastic who started a devotion to Benedict the Moor (now known as St. Benedict the Black). A traveling display was developed and students visited many friars in the province, educating them on the issues and soliciting support for the charitable cause that the students were promoting. For many students at the Holy Name College in Silver Spring, Maryland, this was their first entree into social action.

The marriage of politics and conservative theology was still very new for Catholics, so there wasn't a surge of Catholic involvement in the Civil Rights movement. In the North, the friars, assisted by Third Order Franciscans, started inter-racial understanding groups. The focus of these groups was to go to parish gatherings and make presentations on Church teachings, desegregation, and civil rights. Although the groups were made up of white Catholics, some meetings became very violent and sometimes the Third Order presenters had tomatoes thrown at them. The friars were willing to take the risk and went forward with the program. In fact, it was due to leadership of the North American Federation of the Third Order of Saint Francis that Dr. King was presented with the St. Francis Peace Medal in 1963.

---

[13]James H. Cone, *Martin and Malcolm and America: A Dream or A Nightmare* (Maryknoll, NY: Orbis Books, 1991), 66-67.

There was significant opposition by many Catholics who wrote mean-spirited letters, with some containing charges of communism. In Dr. King's acceptance speech, he commented: "This is the first time that I have had the good fortune, the pleasure and opportunity to receive an award from a Catholic group."[14]

Based on St. Francis' conviction regarding ministry to the poor, the Holy Name Province in New York decided to open a ministry in Harlem. Six Friars were sent to live and work among the people and find out what the community saw as its needs. As a result, *Project Create* was opened in 1967 (ed. note: see article by William Margraff); today one friar still remains.

I don't want to leave you with the false impression that embracing integration was God's solution for America. In response to the U.S. Bishops statement calling for an end to segregation, many Black Catholic parishes in the South merged with the neighboring white Catholic parish as a means of fostering integration. This had a negative impact on future involvement of the Friars, who withdrew from the Black parishes so as to not impede the progress of integration. Since there were fewer parishes to work in, the friars lost interest in Black ministry because there was nothing available which would replace the parish experience. Incidentally, nobody asked Black parishioners if they wanted to merge with a white parish. In merging, they lost the only institution they were in charge of, moving to a surrounding where they were invisible.

Another dilemma occurred concerning the interracial groups. Very few were reading the signposts of change in the Black community. On the horizon were the cultural awareness movement and the development of self-help groups. The inter-racial understanding groups did not see a role for themselves in the new environment and stopped meeting. On the positive side, the National Black Catholic Clergy Caucus and the National Black Sisters' Conference were born and became the new spokespersons for the struggle for justice inside the Church. It was unfortunate that the discussion circles discontinued, because both groups were needed to expand the understanding of racial interaction.[15]

---

[14]Dr. King's Acceptance Speech at the presentation of the 1963 St. Francis Peace Medal by The North American Federation of the Third Order of Saint Francis.

[15]The writer would like to acknowledge the oral testimonies of the following friars who contributed to this article: Rev. Roy Gasnick, O.F.M., Rev. James E. Goode, O.F.M., Rev.

Much has happened since Daniel Rudd and his followers brought the issue of civil rights for the African American community to the Church in the United States, yet much remains to be done. The rapid increase in the number of Black Catholics that occurred in the 1970s indicates a concomitant growth in importance of the Black Catholic community. (A 1975 statistical profile reported 916,854 Black Catholics in the United States.) The Bishops set the stage for a national dialogue on race in their 1974 Pastoral Letter "Brothers and Sisters To Us." The Bishops wrote: "Racism is a sin: a sin that divides the human family, blots out the image of God among specific members of that family, and violates the fundamental human dignity of those called to be children of the same Father."[16]

By 1984, the number of Black bishops had grown to ten. By that same year, the Black Catholic population had increased by over 375,000 to a total of 1,294,103 – an increase of 41% – but Black Catholics still felt a sense of isolation.[17] In a challenge to African American Catholics, the Bishops described themselves as a "sign among other signs that the Black Catholic community has now come of age" and urged Black Catholics to take up the task of evangelizing the un-churched among them.[18]

The Present

This call to action led to the re-development of a new Congress Movement in 1987. The National Black Catholic Pastoral Plan addressed some of the same issues presented 100 years ago. The plan says that successful evangelization of African Americans requires the following elements:

- Know African American Catholic history
- Lift up the strengths of African American cultural styles, behaviors, and cultural qualities
- Develop indigenous leadership
- Speak out on behalf of the poor

Francis Gorman, O.F.M., Rev. Neil J. O'Connell, O.F.M., and Rev. Ben Taylor, O.F.M.

[16]"Brothers and Sisters to Us," U.S. Bishops' Pastoral Letter on Racism in Our Day, Nov. 14, 1979, 3.

[17]James Cavendish, "Church-based Community Activity: A Comparison of Black and White Catholic Congregations" (University of South Florida, June, 1999).

[18]"What We Have Seen and Heard," A Pastoral Letter on Evangelization from the Black Bishops of the United States, 1984, 2.

The Seventh National Black Catholic Congress in 1992 continued organizing Black Catholics by broadening its agenda to address specific problems of the Black community. Strengthening African American families was the focus of this Congress. A comprehensive "family enrichment" program was developed, and, for the first time, delegates identified a public policy platform which met the needs of their families. The Eighth National Black Catholic Congress in August, 1997 returned to the theme of evangelization, in response to Pope John Paul II's emphasis on New Evangelization. The goal of the Eighth Congress was that participants would feel the special sense of being sent as prophetic voices, speaking on behalf of the Lord so as to heal, to mend, to comfort, to build, to restore, and to create a New Kingdom of justice, love, and peace. Another component of this Congress was the dedication of the "Our Mother of Africa Chapel" at the Basilica of the National Shrine of the Immaculate Conception in Washington, D.C.[19]

The Congress movement appears to have achieved modest success in realizing goals of increased visibility, the development of culturally-relevant evangelization programs and an articulation of Black Catholic concerns. In some parishes and programs there is evidence of changes that have been made to make the Church more "welcoming" to the African American community. As an evangelization strategy, considerable pressure is placed upon Catholic leaders to be inclusive in programs, staff, and policy-making.

The National Black Catholic Congress movement of the 20th century reflects the newly-acquired sense of ethnic pride and cultural identity that has stimulated increased action. The Congress movement gives a voice to Black Catholics while dealing as well with the ugly scar of racism. However, even with a substantial increase in African American self-determination and self-confidence, the paradigm has not shifted for the masses of African Americans. More Black men than ever languish in prisons. Black academic achievement still lags behind that of whites. And suicides among young Black men have risen sharply. African Americans make up 13% of the population, yet Black people only earn 7% of the income and control only 3% of the wealth. According to the U.S. Census Bureau, about half of all Black children are being reared in female-headed households. The Black unemployment rate, according to the Bureau of Labor Statistics, is 8.7%, about 2.3 times greater than the rate for Whites. One-third of Black men of

---

[19] See the NBCC website at www.nbccongress.org

unemployment rate, according to the Bureau of Labor Statistics, is 8.7%, about 2.3 times greater than the rate for Whites. One-third of Black men of college age are in the criminal justice system.

It saddens me to say that despite the issuance of the Bishops' Pastoral "Brothers and Sisters To Us" in 1979, and the 1988 issuance of the document entitled "The Church and Racism" by the Pontifical Commission on Social Justice, many Roman Catholics remain totally unaware of the Church's teachings which demand that we recognize African Americans, Hispanics, Asian Americans, and Native Americans. Archbishop James P. Lyke, O.F.M., former Archbishop of Atlanta, said a long time ago that Black Catholic Christians would be second-class citizens of the Church until they "take their place in leadership beside their brothers and sisters of whatever race or national origin." But today it is estimated that less than one percent of American priests – 270 Black Catholic priests – are available for parish ministry. A recent study by the Center for Applied Research (CARA) reveals that there are approximately 300 Black Sisters. Blacks are not that much better represented among those entering into ministerial formation. Blacks currently account for 4% of diaconate candidates (CARA 1999), and 1.2% of lay parish ministers (Murnion and DeLambo 1999), and 3% of students in lay ministry formation (CARA 1999). Again this suggests that the Church is slow to change and a substantial under-representation, if not a complete lack of representation, of Blacks in Church ministerial leadership is the reality today.

The following letter was written by an African American student who attended a Catholic college. Although not written to me, I believe that the letter gives us a sense of the African American experience of Church in the United States. The letter states:

> I would like to tell you a little bit about myself and about my experience at Saint Ambrose College. Saint Ambrose is a good college which gave me an excellent opportunity to learn and to sharpen my skills. I probably would not have had that opportunity had I not gone there, but my college years at Saint Ambrose were not easy ones. You see, Saint Ambrose is an all male, all white Catholic college. I was one of five Black students there and it was very difficult at times for me to feel at home at Saint Ambrose. There was no question in my mind that there was a subtle racism on the part of

the student body and faculty which the [other] Black students and I felt. I experienced this many times when the priests and brothers would spend more time with the white students and when they seemed to be getting all the attention. It was also difficult for me to relate socially to the students at the college. Oftentimes I found myself completely lost, not knowing how to respond when they weren't very friendly. There were occasions when we would get together and I would fake songs that the other students were singing just to show that I was part of the group. I had to struggle to get through math and English, especially when I had little or no help, but I was able to make good grades. But when graduation day came around, I held my head up high because I was so proud of myself. I knew as I marched down the aisle that I had accomplished more than any other student there because I had made it against odds which the other students did not face. Don't get me wrong, Saint Ambrose is an excellent school. It just has to clean up its act.[20]

This is a letter which most African Americans who are Catholic could have written. It's a letter that sums up, in effect, the experience of African-Americans within the institutional Church. It's an experience that is, more often than not, characterized by indifference or hostile reactions, gestures, attitudes, and platitudes on the part of whites which spell rejection and exclusion. This letter, and the stories and examples of courageous action, along with the historical narrative that preceded it, highlight the resiliency of a faithful group of people. The most important part of the young man's story is the last part, for it tells the whole story; this young man at Saint Ambrose College, like other African American Catholics, recognized this reality for what it was and was able to work through it. He made it through and when he graduated he held his head up high because he felt he had accomplished more than any other student there. It's a struggle to be an African American Catholic, but we love the faith and have remained faithful.

---

[20]From an address made by Bishop John H. Ricard, S.S.J., to Catholic Foundations in 1989. Bishop Ricard has served as Bishop in the dioceses of Baltimore and Tallahassee-Pensacola.

The Future

What does this all mean? In recent years the Church has turned its attention to responding to numerous issues affecting ministry today. No longer is the African American community the only cultural community to minister to but now is joined by Latinos, Asians, Pacific-Islanders, and immigrants from various parts of the world. This isn't necessarily a negative factor, but it does pose some concern for African American Catholics. With the mass exodus of many Catholics to the suburbs, the Church has focused much of its attention and resources in serving this growing population and its accompanying needs for larger churches and schools. The personnel crunch within the Church, the smaller pool of priests and religious to choose from, new policies for making assignments coupled with new criteria for keeping parishes open – all of these factors – place many African American parishes, schools and ministries in direct competition with each other, and in some cases constitutes a threat to their very survival, with respect to staffing by religious congregations. Perhaps the largest issues to be dealt within this new reality are fewer personnel, an aging population, and recognition that there are certain skills needed to minister to a variety of cultures. Although there is the perception that mainstream America has opened its doors to African Americans, many other doors remain shut. That such masses of people continue to live in poverty constitutes a major problem for local Churches in their ministry to African Americans. One out of three Blacks still lives in poverty, and there is less access to services. The U.S. Catholic Bishops' Economic Pastoral, "Economic Justice for All," insists that concern for poor people and the destitute is at the core of our social teachings. When we talk about poor people in the U.S. today we are talking about African Americans, Latinos, and the rural population. They have the greatest needs, but they are also the weakest voice and have little influence.

My challenge to the Franciscan Family is to build bridges with the African American community. Put this at the top of the Franciscan agenda. Franciscans can be a sacred instrument in leading the nation against racism. The Franciscan charism is needed and wanted in the Black Community. As Franciscans and partners you have a certain appeal. Your founders were deeply involved in pastoral work, not just parishes or schools. An estimated 4% of U.S. Catholics, about 2.5 million people, are African American. The largest numbers of African-Americans live in the archdioceses or dioceses of

New Orleans; Brooklyn; Chicago; Washington; Lafayette, Louisiana; Baltimore; St. Louis; Philadelphia; Houston, and Louisville, Kentucky. There are opportunities to start something, some creative ministries, but most importantly, there must be a desire to work among the people.

Two examples confirm this, both found in New York City. One deals with drugs and substance abuse, Project Create, and the other provides counseling, support and education to the Black Community, Solid Ground. There is also the National Apostolate for Life. These are examples of programs that meet a need and a Franciscan spirit was given to them. If you are committed to a multicultural ministry, be willing to experience the poverty and challenges of urban life. There needs to be a certain comfortableness with the Community. St. Francis provided a wonderful example of this strategy by living in the houses of the people and listening to their issues and concerns. Take six or seven months to meet people, get to know one another and let relationships develop. When asked what should men and women from the cultures of the world who come to the Black Community do, Sister Thea Bowman, a Franciscan Sister of Perpetual Adoration, Ph.D., responded by saying: "If you are serious about understanding [African Americans] understand their history, their experience, their culture, their heritage, their art, their music, their styles of prayer, their styles of meeting, their songs, their dances, and their modalities of relationships."[21]

As Franciscans you possess unique qualities that help make reconciliation a part of your lives and ministry. Society doesn't realize how strained the relationships are between the cultures and ethnic groups. The Franciscan charism could build a bridge over the racial divide created by hundreds of years of pain and injustice and racial alienation. "Lord, make me an instrument of your peace" - the prayer attributed to St. Francis - is widely known and prayed throughout the Black community. Speaking out and working with the marginalized is a legacy of Franciscan ministry. Specific issues may change, but the disparities remain. Franciscans can bring that same type of commitment and zeal to eliminating racism. No longer can you be silent on these issues and vocal on other life issues; both are important to the dignity of humankind. In the article, "She Made the Bishops Dance," the author reflected on the common dream of Sr. Thea and her friend Sr.

---

[21]Celestine Cepress, FSPA, ed., *Sister Thea Bowman: Shooting Star Selected Writings and Speeches* (Winona, MN: St. Mary's Press, 1993), 106-07.

Dolores Harrall, that "the mission of the church, to which we sisters have committed ourselves, the option for the poor inspires us to believe that a 'community without walls' is the community we are shaping. It is no easy task. Whole lifetimes are absorbed in the struggle."[22] This, too, is my dream: that Franciscans will become active partners with the African American community. The dream never explodes or dries up like a raisin in the sun, but in my dream, we march on 'til victory is won. Blessed Assurance!

Beverly Carroll is the Executive Director of the Secretariat for African American Catholics at the U.S. Conference of Catholic Bishops in Washington, D.C. She has worked for the Conference since 1987, and also serves on the board of the National Black Catholic Congress in Baltimore, Maryland. Ms. Carroll has received an honorary doctorate from Siena College in Loudonville, New York.

---

[22]Christian Koontz, RSM, *Thea Bowman: Handing on Her Legacy* (Kansas City, MO: Sheed and Ward, 1991), 54-57.

Questions For Reflection

1. Why is being familiar with the "image of God" concept critical to positive aspects of selfhood for African Americans?

2. What does our Catholic social teaching say about the sin of racism?

3. Are Franciscans a part of the solution to getting the issue resolved? How?

4. What steps should be taken to build cross-cultural relationships? How did St. Francis do it?

5. How can the Franciscan Family spread the Gospel in the African American Community today?

An Alternate Vision of Society:
The Legacy And Challenge Of the Third Order Franciscan Way Of Life

Patricia Keefe, O.S.F.

Francis of Assisi's vision about society attracted large numbers of followers during his lifetime and even today. There are more members of the varied ways of life belonging to the Franciscan Family than to any other Catholic Religious group. This chapter briefly traces the development of Third Order Franciscans as an urban phenomenon. Given a tradition of responding to the challenge of Gospel life within the city, Third Order Franciscans in the United States are faced with the question of living that heritage in the 21st Century is the question to be faced.

The first section of the chapter will focus briefly on the life of Third Order Franciscans in Medieval Europe. The second section picks up how the tradition was exemplified in the experience of Third Order Franciscans in the United States up to the 1970's. The third section is on the persistent pattern of poverty in United States' cities and what might be the challenge for Third Order Franciscans in this cultural context.

Early Third Order Franciscans in Medieval European Cities

One challenge facing the study of the early Third Order Franciscans is that historically they were called a variety of different names. We who are accustomed to the way religious life is structured in the Roman Catholic Church today need to step outside our own experience to grasp what it was like at a time when the only understanding of women's religious life was that they were to be enclosed in monasteries. The early followers of Francis were generally known as Penitents. "Tertiaries" and "Third Order" were appellations that came later.

Another reality which was evident when the Franciscan movement was born was the desire of women to live a religious life, an option widely available to men but not to women unless they agreed to enclosure. When a community founded by a male leader was first formed, provision was often made for women to be admitted to a women's branch, but within a century after founding, this arrangement would be prohibited.[1] Along with this pattern was the determination of the Church to consider as religious only those women who chose strict enclosure.

The penitential movement was essentially a lay movement and therefore included women. It seems from the sources that Francis became an inspiration to the growth of this movement, which pre-dated his conversion. The first version of Francis's *Letter to the Faithful*, also referred to as an *Exhortation to the Brothers and Sisters of Penance*, dates from around 1215.[2] By 1221, this way of life became more structured with Cardinal Hugolino's *Memoriale Proposito* and was approved as a Rule by the Church in 1289 when Pope Nicholas IV issued *Supra Montem*.[3] This Rule applied both to penitents living under vows and in community or in hermitages and to those living in their own homes.

It is in the *Memoriale* and specifically in the *Rule of 1289* that guidelines for those seeking a life of penance emerged:

1) Following a simple life-style, as seen in the specifications about clothing: status and prestige through clothing were to be avoided.

2) Provisions made for prayer in common and in connection with the Universal Church: daily Mass and fasting. Penitents met in local churches.

3) Nonviolence: Penitents were not to bear arms or to take oaths. An exception to this principle was already evident by 1289 when bearing arms for the defense of the Church was made an exception. Oaths were to be avoided since allegiance was to the Church, not civil authority.

4) Goods, i.e. money, were to be shared with those who were poor.

The significance of these early developments is that choosing the penitential life meant choosing a way of life which was in significant ways an alternative

---

[1]Patricia Ranft, *Women and the Religious Life in Pre-modern Europe* (New York: St. Martin's Press, 1996), 46-59.

[2]*Francis of Assisi The Saint: Early Documents*, vol. 1, eds. Regis J Armstrong, O.F.M. Cap., Wayne Hellmann, O.F.M. Conv., and William J. Short, O.F.M. (New York: New City Press, 1999), 41-44. Hereafter, *FA:ED*. See Roland J. Faley T.O.R.," The Letter to All the Faithful-Recensio prior" from *A Biblical-theological View of Penance and Its Present Day Expression* (Greensburg, PA: Charles M. Henry Printing Company, 1979). Also available from the Franciscan Federation in *Sources for the Study of the TOR Rule*.

[3]Robert M. Stewart, *"De Illis qui faciunt Penitentiam" The Rule of the Secular Franciscan Order: Origins, Development, Interpretation* (Rome: Capuchin Historical Institute, 1991), 203 -16. See also: Mariano D' Alatri. "Origin of the *Rule of Nicholas IV*: Historical Aspects." *Greyfriars Review*, 4/3 (1990): 107-18.

approach to the society in which those choosing a life of penance found themselves. In fact, the primitive Rule for the penitents came about because civil authorities were pressuring the tertiaries to take an oath to bear arms when the civic leaders commanded.[4]

While the Rule of 1289 was followed by both penitents living in their own homes and those who lived in communities, each form of life began to be distinctive. In a papal document, *Nimis Patenter*, dated June 25, 1227, Pope Gregory IX, the former Cardinal Hugolino dei Conti, refers to the existence at that time of the secular Franciscans and those who lived either in hermitages or in community. Pazzelli describes the various manifestations of penitential life, specifically noting that some of those in small groups lived near hospitals where they engaged in spiritual and corporal works of mercy.[5]

The reference to Third Order groups living near hospitals is significant in light of the practice of charity toward those who were poor during the centuries when the Franciscan movement was growing in number. Hospitals and hospices were the primary institutions serving poor people even before the time of Francis and Clare.[6] Very early, in 1216, Jacques de Vitry refers to Franciscan women living together near the cities in various hospices and living by the labor of their hands.[7] After becoming acquainted with Friars Minor in 1232, Agnes of Prague built a hospital dedicated to Francis.[8] In 1237 the direction of this hospital was entrusted to the Confraternity of the Crosiers of the Red Star thus showing Agnes' connection to the penitential movement.

Outreach to those who were poor and in need of care also characterized the Third Order Regular men's communities. Pazzelli describes the Tertiaries in Reggio Emilia in 1238 as visiting the poor in their homes. They

---

[4]Raffaele Pazzeli, T.O.R. *The Third Order Regular of St. Francis Through the Centuries*, trans. Aidan Mullaney, T.O.R. (Steubenville, Ohio: Franciscan University Press, 1994), 6.

[5]Pazzelli, 20.

[6]Michel Mollat, *The Poor in the Middle Ages: An Essay in Social History*, trans. Arthur Goldhammer (New Haven: Yale University Press, 1986), 93: "Charitable fraternities were founded on lay initiative in the cities, and some of these were eventually transformed into permanent congregations. One of the best known of these was the fraternity founded by Gui of Montpellier around 1160. This was a hospital society dedicated to the care of the poor, the sick, and abandoned children."

[7]*Lettres de Jacques de Vitry*, ed. R.B.C. Huygens (Leiden: E.J. Brill, 1960), 75-76.

[8]*Francis and Clare: The Complete Works*, trans. and intro. by Regis J. Armstrong, O.F.M. Cap., and Ignatius Brady, O.F.M. (New York: Paulist Press, 1982), 189.

also built a large house to serve as a free dispensary for medicine and as a place of storage of food for the poor.[9]

Angelina of Montegiove (1357-1435), established the prototype for Third Order Franciscan Women living in an autonomous congregation with more than one house, each governed by an elected leader. When Angelina arrived in Foligno, where she began to form a Third Order Regular community, she was given a site near a hospital.[10] Under Angelina's leadership, other Third Order communities formed, based on her model of community living and service to those who were poor. Those in Poland, which were founded with the support of Bernardine of Siena and John Capistran, were connected to Angelina. The foundations at Cracow, 1454-1594, were involved in care of the sick and of the poor.[11]

Another significant Franciscan was Angela Merici who eventually founded the Ursulines. Angela was born about 1474. She joined a Third Order community, probably at Desenzano, in the convent of San Bernardino. Thereafter, Angela received requests (even from Pope Clement VII) to organize charities.[12] In a study of Franciscan elements in Angela's spirituality, Carolyn Brockland points to Angela's reputation as a peacemaker dating from her early years.[13]

The works of the early Third Order communities were located in cities because with the change from the feudal system to the rise of economies based on money, poor persons became much more numerous in cities. While Francis and Clare went outside the *commune* of Assisi to minister in the hospitals for the lepers, their followers generally found the poor and outcast in cities.[14] We see that these early examples of Third Order Regular

---

[9]Pazzelli, 66.

[10]Roberta A. McKelvie, O.S.F., *Retrieving a Living Tradition Angelina of Montegiove* (St. Bonaventure, NY: Franciscan Institute Publications, 1997), 77.

[11]McKelvie, 124-25.

[12]Angela "spent years working with a group of lay Christians to relieve misery brought to Brescia, a city near her birthplace, by the French invasion of Italy. She helped to organize orphanages and refuges for prostitutes, and she worked in a hospital for incurables, the only hospital that would accept Brescia's increasing numbers of syphilitics." See Ann White, "Serpents and Doves: The Company of St. Ursula," *Review for Religious* 58/1 (1999): 42-47.

[13]Carolyn M. Brockland, O.S.U., "Elements of Franciscan Spirituality in the Life and Writings of Angela Merici," *Greyfriars Review*, 12/2 (1998): 211-39. The article first appeared in *Analecta TOR* 28/161 (1997): 439-66.

[14]Chiara Frugoni, *A Distant City Images of Urban Experience in the Medieval World*, trans. William McCuaig, Princeton, NJ: Princeton University Press, 1991. Frugoni finds in the art of the medieval period that cities were seen as places of civilization where the government and the church were present while outside the walls lurked dangers and darkness, an uncivilized world. See also Michael Himes, "Returning to Our Ancestral Lands," *Review for Religious* 59/1 (2000):

life, characterized by community life and service, continue in the tradition down through the centuries even though there were many efforts to impose strict enclosure for women's communities. The brief vision of life laid out in the Rule of 1289 was given flesh in the way the Third Order Regular communities focused on service to those who were poor. The vision also included the way in which they related in service.

The development which eventually led to the separation of the Third Order Secular and Regular was somewhat fluid until Pope Nicholas V published the bull *Pastoralis Officii* in 1447 in response to requests from penitential groups all over Italy: "The office of Shepherd moves us to turn our loving care to the religious of the Third Order of Penance who live in Italy. We desire to grant them a stable government so that, in removing obstacles, they can the more quickly give their attention to divine service and contemplation."[15]

Francis had a deep conviction based on the Gospel that all of God's creatures are brothers and sisters. The novelty of this insight can be seen more clearly in light of attitudes toward poverty during the Middle Ages. Theological understanding current during the 12th and 13th centuries included a strong emphasis on the Gospel texts which spoke to how difficult it would be for the rich to get to heaven. Vivid images of hell and purgatory worked to convey a strong reason to share one's wealth with those who were poor. One medieval scholar, Michel Mollat writes:

> What all the unfortunates had in common was their humiliation and dependency and it was only from the height of a spiritual vantage that the value in such a fate could be perceived. For, in yet another paradox of poverty, the poor formed what might be an "order" or estate in the economy of salvation.[16]

Mollat notes in the introduction to his book that the problem of poverty in the Middle Ages was complex and ambiguous: the biblical and gospel traditions, occasionally broken but always revived, retained a kind of latent power, like that of a dominant virus. The metaphor makes clear the explo-

---

7-25, especially pages 14-15, where Himes notes that Francis, Clare and Dominic emerged in response to the movement of peoples to larger cities where clergy were small in number.

[15]Pazzelli, 106.

[16]Mollat, 70.

sive force found in Francis of Assisi's proclamation of the dignity of the poor and of the duty to restore that dignity. This was a new turn in the dialectic of happiness and suffering.[17] Mollat further describes how the preaching and teaching of the Franciscans and Dominicans on the duty to help the poor was augmented by the work of the Third Orders and beguines, which he says were deeply involved in charitable endeavors.[18]

Francis' revolutionary insight is seen clearly in the Admonitions, particularly those relating to appropriation. (*Admonitions* 2:3, 3:1, 4:3, 5:7, 7:4, 8:3, 17:1 and 18:2)[19] Francis turned upside down the prevalent notions in his world concerning the need to uphold one's honor at all costs, taking revenge, accumulating wealth, and having power over others. He saw that appropriation of anything as one's own constituted a denial of the fundamental equality of all creatures and of God as the great Almsgiver. That this tradition remains alive in our time is seen in Leonardo Boff for one, who describes Francis' insight this way: "There is an umbilical cord between persons that cannot be cut due to the fact of being permanently tied to God and in the hands of the Father of goodness."[20]

Jean François Godet-Calogeras has pointed out that the relationship of brothers/sisters is the "program" for Franciscans, the way of life that flows from our equality in having nothing, of being creatures of one God.[21] And another Franciscan scholar, David Flood, O.F.M., has gone back to the lives of the first friars to discover the radical roots of the tradition which has come down to us. Because Francis and the men who followed him were in a society which considered itself Christian, they gave attention to how Gospel living was different from that society. At the core of the difference, Flood finds, was their radical identification and inclusiveness of all within a society where the haves and the have-nots were not considered equal. By identifying with the "riffraff" and doing so by choice, the early friars confronted Assisi's belief that alms need only be given to the "deserving."[22]

---

[17]Mollat, 11.
[18]Mollat, 127.
[19]*FA:ED I*, 128-37, *passim*.
[20]Leonardo Boff, *St. Francis: A Model for Human Liberation*, trans. John W. Diercksmeier (New York: Crossroad Publishing, 1982), 103.
[21]Jean Francois Godet-Calogeras, *Proposito: Presentation on the Evangelical Life*, Franciscan Federation of the Brothers and Sisters of the United States, 1984.
[22]David Flood, *Work for Every One: Francis of Assisi and the Ethic of Service* (Quezon City, Philippines: CCFMC Office for Asia/Oceania, Inter-Franciscan Center) 1997. See also Bernard

These deeply held convictions of Francis pervaded the vision of the Third Order with its focus on service. Foundational in community and service were Francis' insight that each and all of us are children of the one God who is all good:

> Let us refer all good
> to the Lord, God Almighty and Most High,
> acknowledge that every good is His,
> and thank Him,
> "From Whom all good comes,
> for everything."
> May He,
> the Almighty and Most High,
> the only true God,
> have, be given, and receive
> all honor and respect,
> all praise and blessing,
> all thanks and glory,
> to Whom all good belongs,
> He Who alone is good.[23]

Francis did not leave the world which as God's creation is good; he left the values of the world.[24] Raoul Manselli examined the early Franciscan documents for his analysis of Francis' status after his conversion. He concluded that in the Testament, Francis "states very clearly that his conversion consisted in a reversal of values, not in a change of juridical status." He was "passing from the social status of a rich merchant to that of the humblest and poorest, with no legal protection."[25] His significance in his own time and in the centuries following relates to this belief, a belief which is an alternative vision for how we can live together as brothers and sisters.

McGinn, *The Flowering of Mysticism: Men and Women in the New Mysticism 1200-1350* (New York: Crossroad Publishing, 1998), 41-69.

[23]*FA:ED I, The Earlier Rule*, XXII: 17-18.

[24]Ilia Delio, O.S.F., *Following Christ in the Second Axial Period.* Work in progress, 1999.

[25]Raoul Manselli, "Francis of Assisi and Lay People Living in the World: Beginning of the Third Order?" trans. Edward Hagman, O.F.M. Cap., *Greyfriars Review* 11/1 (1997): 42.

Third Order Regular Franciscans in the United States: Beginnings to 1970s

Given these roots, we now look at how the tradition stayed alive in the new world, starting in the mid-nineteenth century when Third Order Regular Franciscan Brothers arrived in the United States from Ireland in 1846. At about the same time a small group of Secular Franciscan women and men arrived from Germany.

Margaret Slowick, O.S.F., has studied the Third Order communities which began then and those which developed over the next 150 years in the United States. While the depth of life for these congregations has yet to be studied, the listing of the communities and where and how they began itself documents their commitment to service. All but one of twenty-nine communities founded between 1847 and 1877 were established to work with the primarily German and Irish immigrants of that time.[26] Not only were the Catholic immigrants needy, they also were subject to anti-Catholic bigotry which characterized the United States during these years. Consequently, these founders and members may well have seen themselves as counter-cultural in their service.

The question can be raised, however, whether the Third Order Regular Franciscan communities, especially those which originated in the United States without connection to existing Franciscan communities in Europe, were consciously aware of the Franciscan vision for society. Was their service in any way different from other communities founded in the United States during this period of time? The Rochester, Minnesota, Third Order Regular Franciscan Congregation, begun in 1877, might be seen as typical of those that began in the United States during the 19th century. The Congregation was certainly involved in service from its origins in Owatonna, Minnesota. It also had to face anti-Catholic bias and was counter-cultural in light of the strong ecumenical focus in its service. A story is told about the anti-Catholic bias which impinged on the operation of St. Mary's Hospital which the Sisters completed in 1889 and where they closely worked with the Doctors Mayo who were not Catholic. "Ardent Protestants would have none of an institution that was managed by black robed nuns and in which there

---

[26]Margaret A. Slowick, O.S.F., "Franciscan Third Order Regular Congregations in the United States: Origins and Early Years," thesis submitted to St. Bonaventure University, St. Bonaventure, NY, 1999, 6.

was a chapel set aside for the exercise of popery."[27] Dr. Mayo enlisted the help of an esteemed Presbyterian whom he named as nominal superintendent of St. Mary's in order to quiet the furor. St. Mary's served all regardless of religion. Mother Alfred Moes's belief that sickness knew no religion was based, it would seem, on a core Franciscan value, relating to all as brothers and sisters.

Before the Second Vatican Council, there was relatively little attention paid to Franciscan traditions and its specific spirituality in the Rochester Franciscan Community and presumably others like it. Many of the retreat directors provided by the Congregation for the members were Jesuits. The formation program was largely based on the 1927 Third Order Rule, which was a boiler-plate Rule much like those of other Congregations. In the Congregation's Constitutions as late as the 1960's, these were presented as rules to make it easier to live together in community and as a way to earn heaven.

The 1927 Third Order Rule was written without any input from Franciscans. The early commitment to non-violence, seen in the penitents' exemption from bearing arms, was lost much earlier, at the time the Church was employing force for its own needs. The vestiges of the Church's constantly reiterated concern that all religious women had to be enclosed were clearly present in the ways Third Order Women, even in the United States, were separated from the "world." Life focused on community living and striving to attain perfection. As late as 1969 reference was made in a letter from a priest to the leadership of the Rochester Franciscans that "strict enclosure" was to be observed by a sister teaching in his parish. It can be said, however, that the 1927 Rule helped protect the Third Order Regular (TOR) religious women from strict enclosure. Roberta A. McKelvie, a Bernardine Franciscan from Reading, Pennsylvania, referred to the same kind of experi-

---

[27]Helen Clapesattle, *The Doctors Mayo* (Minneapolis, MN: University of Minnesota Press, 1941), 136. See also Carol K. Coburn and Martha Smith. *Spirited Lives: How Nuns Shaped American Culture 1836-1920* (Chapel Hill: University of N. Carolina Press, 1999), 42: "In 1830, *The* Protestant began publication with the objective 'to inculcate Gospel doctrines against Romist corruptions . . . to maintain the purity and sufficiency of the Holy Scriptures against Monkish Traditions,' asserting that no article would be printed unless it promoted this goal.... Communities of women religious often took the brunt of anti-Catholic prejudice. As women who lived and worked in all-female environments, created and maintained schools and institutions in the public domain, wore "mysterious" distinctive clothing, and took vows of chastity and obedience while rejecting heterosexual marriage, nuns elicited a gamut of Protestant fantasies."

ence in her presentation in the "Rebirth of a Charism" program of the Franciscan Federation. When she said: "If you keep the Rule…" all of the mostly TOR crowd said instantly: "…the Rule will keep you." This response was in reference to the 1927 Rule which governed TOR communities from that date until 1982. McKelvie also spoke of the aspects of enclosure that clung to the TOR communities in the United States. For example, the American foundation of the community began in 1894 when four sisters from Poland began teaching in Mt. Carmel, Pennsylvania; in 1895 they moved to Reading and began to care for orphans. At first connected to the Bernardine community in Poland, the Reading community became independent under the leadership of Mother Hedwig who began her eighteen-year leadership of the community in 1912.[28] About communities like these, Margaret Susan Thompson has written: "To assume, then, that every community designated as "Franciscan" also intentionally embodied a Franciscan charism requires an enormous leap of faith; in fact, even some founders who wanted to be "Franciscan" sometimes began by organizing themselves by another Rule."[29]

Franciscans were not the only communities somewhat disconnected from their founders' charisms. Many communities founded in the United States were functional, i.e., they began in response to a need with little attention paid to spirituality. "A basic problem was that canon law rather than the gospel law of love was set up as the ideal" wrote Josephine Marie Peplinski in her two-volume history of the Sisters of St. Joseph of the Third Order of St. Francis. Benedictines met the same fate, "fading into the mass of apostolic orders."[30]

While the Third Order Regular emerged from the same roots as the lay movement of the Third Order Secular, TOR communities in the United States were not significantly different than those of other traditions. Canon Law had successfully "homogenized" religious life for women. Third Order Franciscans were not obviously distinguishable from other apostolic communities. Some aspects of the charism of the Third Order were lost temporarily to functionalism. Emerging in the 1950's however were stirrings of a retrieval of what was distinctively Franciscan. In 1952, The Franciscan Sis-

---

[28]Slowick, 84.

[29]Margaret Susan Thompson, "Charism or Deep Story? Towards Understanding Better the 19th Century Origins of American Women's Congregations," *Review for Religious* 58/3 (1999): 237.

[30]Thompson, 239-40.

ters' Educational Conference, an offshoot of the Franciscan Educational Conference begun by the Friars Minor in the early 1900's, had this express purpose: "to study and to bear witness to the living, developing spirit of Saint Francis as it encounters the challenges of our times and the contemporary needs of Franciscan Sisters."[31]

The Second Vatican Council marked the beginning of change in Third Order Regular Franciscan life. With the Council's call for Congregations to return to their roots came a vast explosion in scholarship based on the charism and vision of the founders of Third Order Congregations. Significantly, there was also the emergence of scholarship based on original sources of the beginnings and medieval development of the Franciscan way of life. The Franciscan Federation consisting of the Third Order Regular of the Sisters and Brothers of the United States was established in 1966 and has served as a focus for scholarship and education in this country since that time.

A key development occurred in 1974 when the Federation sent its president to the Fourth Franciscan Tertiary Inter-Obediential Congress in Madrid, Spain. Unforeseen at the time, this meeting led to the Federation's participation in the international project which would lead to the promulgation of the Third Order Rule in 1982.[32] The Franciscan Federation also was responsible for assisting the recovery of the charism of peace and nonviolence that was buried within the penitential roots of Third Order life. It also chose a concentration on peace and justice when, in 1984, the Federation's Peace and Justice Committee formulated "A Vision of Franciscan Peacemaking." The Prologue reads:

> Franciscan peacemaking begins when we realize that peace is a gift from God, our Creator. Peace grows when we live the Gospel as brothers and sisters with all people, as reconcilers of injustice and in harmony with all God's creatures. Our peacemaking continually arises from the values we profess and live out together.[33]

---

[31]Elise Saggau, O.S.F., "A Short History of the Franciscan Federation 1965-1999" (Washington, DC: The Franciscan Federation, 1995), 2.

[32]Saggau, 7.

[33]Saggau, 12.

Peace and non-violence as a way of life pervade the 1982 *Rule and Life of the Brothers and Sisters*. Many Third Order communities have adopted non-violence and peacemaking in Congregational goals. In 1999, the Rochester Franciscans in Minnesota reaffirmed non-violence as one of four Congregational Challenges: "to foster non-violence as a way of life, personally and communally, confronting violence within ourselves, society and the environment." Many Third Order members support Franciscans International at the United Nations, a project of the Franciscan Family. The goals of Franciscans International are: Care of Creation, Concern for the Poor, and Peacemaking. A recent newsletter had the lead headline: "Franciscans International Takes Major Steps to Eradicate Poverty, To Abolish War."[34]

The development of the Third Order *Rule* and the recovery of the roots of peace and non-violence in the penitential way of life have revitalized the Third Order Regular of the Sisters and Brothers of the United States. By 1994 when the Bishops' Synod on Consecrated Life in the Church issued its *Lineamenta* on the elements of Religious Life, the Federation was able to distinguish the Franciscan way of life as different from the apostolic and monastic models:

> The Franciscan charism is always and everywhere unbounded. In Francis' own words, "The world is our cloister." With Christ, Firstborn of all creation, nothing in creation is untouched by the Spirit of the Lord. Franciscans seek to proclaim the fundamental Goodness of God in all of life and creation. All of life and creation is a gift from God.[35]

Given that recovery and the renewed interest in how the tradition might look in today's culture, the time is right to see what might be our challenge as our society moves into the 21st century.

---

[34]Franciscans International Quarterly Newsletter, XI/3 (July 1999): 1.
[35]Saggau, 25.

Persistent Poverty in the United States:
What is the Challenge to Third Order Franciscans?

Contemporary society in the United States is in some ways dramatically different from that in which Francis and the early penitents lived. Clearly the United States is not a Christian society in the sense that Assisi was. Where Francis' challenge was to a society immersed in a Christian belief system, our challenge exists in a quite different context. Fear of hell and difficulty for the rich getting into heaven if they do not give alms is hardly persuasive in the United States today. What is the same, however, is the conviction that there are *deserving* as well as undeserving poor, and that the haves are qualitatively different from the have-nots. In terms of the unjust economic system which Francis addressed by identifying with the riff-raff, the present system is very similar. How do we address an attitude that holds that some people deserve their poverty? Our Franciscan vocation values service to the poor and a conviction that all are brothers and sisters. Where does that take us as we move into the early part of the 21st century?

An article which appeared in the *St. Paul Pioneer Press* during the hoopla surrounding the 1999 Super Bowl in Miami poignantly describes the crisis in our cities by exposing the realities of a neighborhood within the shadow of the stadium:

In South Beach, with its shrinky-dink miniskirts and Art Deco drunks, a woman in a bikini breezed down Ocean Drive on in-line skates, handing out fliers promoting the official game program of Super Bowl XXXIII. Fifteen minutes away, in a 2 square mile patch of hopelessness called Overtown, Alvin Johnson leaned against a pay telephone, holding a beer in a brown paper bag while chewing on a black plastic straw. The streets were cracked and littered with glass. Nearby windows were covered with bars.[36]

Julian Cobb, a probation office in the juvenile justice system in Dade County, Florida, noted the difference in the Overtown neighborhood since he had grown up there. Riots had erupted in that neighborhood in 1989 af-

---

[36]"Miami parties, but life is far from super in Overtown," *St. Paul Pioneer Press*, Sunday, January 31,1999, 1A and 6A.

ter a police officer shot and killed a black man from Overtown and was later acquitted. Cobb doesn't believe riots would happen now because the "community has been severed at its roots." During the riots the feeling was that the "injustice had happened to everyone." That value system is gone, destroyed in part by the drug culture, a symptom of large social ills.[37]

This is a description of one slice of cultural breakdown; the loss of community, the despair and alienation describe many places in our cities and towns. There are echoes in the important work of Mitchell Dunier, a sociologist who studied people's interactions in a fringe neighborhood near the University of Chicago. Dunier decided to observe the diverse crowd that frequented a Greek owned restaurant in the neighborhood. The *Valois* restaurant had become a "hangout" for folks, mostly single men, who lived in the area which included blacks and whites. Dunier observed that the conversations and interrelationships of the ghetto blacks and the whites at the restaurant showed that their values, hopes and desires were very similar.

Dunier concluded that typical "social theory about urban poverty fails to recognize that the working poor are moral beings that can provide their own role models, at least on moral grounds." Further: "Stable working class and working poor blacks are least visible to sociologists and journalists who move in and out of these neighborhoods at a quick pace."[38] Dunier's work is important because it shows that even though the values of those he observed were similar, blacks felt a growing sense of despair about the changes in their own neighborhood. The changes they saw were the same ones observed in Miami – the loss of a sense of community, of shared values, of equal brother and sisterhood.

Charles Derber paints a wider picture of social ills in the United States. Derber points to extreme individualism, the "take care of No. 1" mentality which is threatening the health and well-being of our society:

> Wilding includes a vast spectrum of self-centered and self-aggrandizing behavior that harms others. A wilding epidemic tears at the social fabric and threatens to unravel society itself, ultimately reflecting the erosion of the social order and the withdrawal of

---

[37]"Miami parties." See also Clarence Thomson, "McKenna is a seasoned practitioner of the telling tale," *National Catholic Reporter* 35/14 (1999): 26-28, for Megan McKenna's description of individualism and its effects in the United States.

[38]Mitchell Dunier, *Slims's Table* (Chicago: University of Chicago Press, 1992), 130, 139.

feeling and commitments from others to oneself, to "number one."[39]

Derber vividly spells out all the ways in which "wilding" is evident at all levels of our society, from the senseless shooting of parents or schoolmates, to the wild excess of Michael Milken on Wall Street. His description of America's new underclass is eerily similar to Cobb's description of the Overtown area of Miami. The new underclass is "physically, economically and socially separated from the rest of the population," "cast off by the rest of society and controlled by police and prisons."[40] The import of Derber's analysis for Franciscans is found in the conclusion to his study:

> But to purge the wilding epidemic, Americans in the 1990s will have to rediscover and refashion a version of the moral dream in order to temper the current fever of individualistic materialism and resurrect civil society. The moral vision will have to be creative because of the new threats that unchecked materialism now poses. It will have to encompass an ecological morality, for we know that the untrammeled materialist is incompatible with planetary survival, becoming a form of wilding directed against nature itself.[41]

Derber captures both the depth of the despair caused by rampant individualism and the vision needed to address it. Third Order Regular members have the vision launched by Francis and Clare. Illia Delio writes of this vision:

> What makes Francis so relevant (in our global age) is not the life of poverty or itinerancy that he opted for; rather it is his loving relationship to all people including non-Christians, his sense of brotherhood to all of creation, and his desire to be Gospel-in-the-world by living in the spirit of compassionate love....Through

---

[39]Charles Derber, *The Wilding of America: How Greed and Violence Are Eroding Our Character* (New York: St. Martin's Press, 1996), 6.

[40]Derber, 139. See also William W. Goldsmith and Edward J. L. Blakely, *Separate Societies* (Philadelphia: Temple University Press, 1992). Derber's reference to police and prisons is documented in David Cole, *Unequal Justice: Race and Class in the American Criminal Justice System* (New York: New City Press, 1999).

[41]Derber, 150.

seeing and feeling the compassion of God, Francis came to see and feel with everyone he encountered and all things of creation.[42]

Our broken world needs this passion. It is this vision that needs to be lived out wherever Third Order Regular Franciscans live. It is this vision that needs to be continually articulated by Franciscan scholars. Both the vision of Francis and Clare and TOR presence in these kinds of neighborhoods are needed in our world.

There are examples of TOR presence in these kinds of neighborhoods. A new Franciscan community has formed in the metropolitan area of Minneapolis-St. Paul, Minnesota, where the Franciscan Brothers of the Poor have ministered among those dying of AIDs and now are opening their doors to the victims of torture. Victims of AIDs and torture are present among the most marginalized, the most excluded in our society. Several TORs have lived in the Uptown area of Chicago for over thirty years, committed to those living in poverty, identifying with their struggles. In 1998, the Franciscan Federation gave its annual award to a TOR sister who had given her life for the developmentally disabled, letting no obstacle stand in the way of their need for decent and home-like living space. In 1999, the award went to a TOR member who was deeply involved in education about the earth and ecology. There are other examples too numerous to name.

At the same time, there is the important work of identifying the alternate vision which Franciscan scholars are engaged in around the world. Derber's conclusion is that an alternate vision is imperative for our world. Articulating the Franciscan vision is a key challenge for members of Third Order Regular communities. The Franciscan Federation in the United States and its counterparts in other countries are doing this essential work. Franciscan Schools of Theology are key contributors to the ongoing exploration of the Franciscan vision. The Third Order Rule, presented to the TOR membership in 1982, was the result of collaborative, international work among the Federations and with other branches of the Franciscan family.

Using current scholarship on the early documents and the lived history of the Third Order, the *Rule* Project identified four fundamental values

---

[42]Ilia Delio, O.S.F., unpublished manuscript, p. 7.

which pervade the alternate vision for society: 1) Conversion to God and neighbor; 2) Poverty; 3) Minority; and 4) Contemplation. Of particular significance for the alternate vision and based on Francis' conviction about all being brothers and sisters is Chapter 5 of the Rule: "The Way to Serve and Work": In exchange for their service or work, they may accept anything necessary for their own temporal needs and for that of their sisters or brothers....Whatever they may have over and above their needs, they are to give to the poor. Let them never want to be over others. Instead they should be servants and subject to every human creature for God's sake" (paragraph 19 in part). Paragraph 29 continues:

> Let the brothers and sisters be gentle, peaceful and unassuming, mild and humble, speaking respectfully to all in accord with their vocation. Wherever they are, or wherever they go throughout the world they should not be quarrelsome, contentious, or judgmental towards others. Rather, it should be obvious that they are "joyful, good-humored," and happy in the Lord as they ought to be. And in greeting others, let them say, "God give you peace."[43]

Having explored briefly the roots of our Franciscan values, how those roots became obscure due to historical circumstances, both those affecting the world wide Church and those affecting the new culture developing in the United States, and how needy our society is for a new vision of brotherhood and sisterhood, what can we say about the challenge of TOR life today at the dawn of the new millennium?

Our world is in some ways like that into which Francis and Clare came with their vision of a world where all were brothers and sisters. They faced and we face an economically unjust system which marginalizes large numbers of people. Into that world they brought an alternate vision and transformed hearts deeply rooted in the Gospel vision. They identified with the poor and marginalized in a physical way moving at first outside the city of Assisi where the poor were concentrated. When the poor moved into the cities, so did the early Franciscans. They welcomed all and saw each person as a brother or sister. As we have given over many of our institutions to lay

---

[43]*Rule and Life of the Brothers and Sisters of the Third Order Regular of St. Francis*, American English Commentary written by Margaret Carney, O.S.F. and Thaddeus Horgan, S.A. (Washington, D.C.: The Franciscan Federation, 1982).

persons, more of us are living more closely with those who are poor. What is needed are transformed hearts deeply rooted in the Gospel vision. Paul Philibert, O.P., has described the emerging model of religious life as transformative:

> In this model there is neither a gap nor a concordance between Gospel and culture but rather a critical engagement of culture by the Gospel. One is called to become a *pneumatorphoros*–a person who is a bearer of God's Spirit-transformative ecology. Holiness is a kind of gift of stability that allows Gospel to illumine and stabilize life so that it can be fruitful in genuine human community and in the world.[44]

Francis and Clare faced a world which was Christian in name but unjust in its economics. We live in a country where Catholic Christians have been the largest single denomination continuously since 1850. Now that Catholic Christians are in the mainstream, Catholics are the largest single denomination in the U.S. Congress. When the Bishops of the United States issued a Pastoral on Economy in which they enunciated principles of a just economy and suggested some possible applications, they were roundly criticized by some Catholics and worse, ignored by the masses. Pondering this reaction, Peter Steinfels has pointed out that over time, the economic system of the world began to appear as "a natural system resembling the natural systems operating in the physical universe." Steinfels further elucidates his point by quoting Joyce Appelby's *Capitalism and a New Social Order*: "Although Europe remained robustly Christian, the idea of a natural economic system was like an entering wedge between God and his created universe."[45] If this analysis is accurate, it accounts not only for the rejection and dismissal of the Bishops' Pastoral on the Economy but also for the much of the dismal condition of the marginalized in our country and in our world.

Francis and Clare saw all of God's creation as one and as all good. There was no separation between work and community. The way the early

---

[44]Father Paul Philibert O.P. "Toward a Transformative Model of Religious Life." *Origins* 20/1 (1999): 12.
[45]Peter Steinfels, "A Lay Vocation in the Marketplace" *Origins*, 29/4 (June 10, 1999): 57-61.

Franciscans lived together was the same as the way they worked with others. Early Third Order Franciscans, from what scholars have been able to reconstruct, were both attracted by this vision and incorporated it into their service among those who were poor.

Our Third Order communities are located in towns and cities where housing is unaffordable for many, where minimum wages fail to provide a livable wage, and where despair and violence reign. Our challenge is to critically engage our culture through our identification as brothers and sisters with those who are poor, by educating and by modeling with transformed hearts. Francis and Clare can lead us because their world was much like ours; their living of the Gospel was transformative. Therein lies the challenge for us, those who follow the Franciscan Way of Life specifically and all who search for a vision on which to found their dreams for a different world where brothers and sisters live together in peace and love.

Patricia Keefe is currently working with the development of the Nonviolent Peaceforce (NP). She is responsible for office administration and outreach in the St. Paul, Minnesota, office of Peaceworkers that houses the project management for the Nonviolent Peaceforce. Patricia holds an MA in Theology and has a *Juris Doctor* degree.

Questions for Reflection

1. As Franciscans revive and revitalize their roots in a nonviolent way of life, how do I/we address the many forms of violence in our own lives, in our society, and in the world?

2. "Without vision the people perish." Is the vision found in the Franciscan tradition one that is viable today? How might that vision affect my personal life and ministry?

3. Francis and Clare saw all of God's creation as good. Does this view characterize my way of being, my choice-making and relating day-by-day?

Crime and Punishment:
A Restorative Justice Philosophy

Herbert A. Johnson

"Do not forget to entertain strangers, for by so doing some people have entertained angels without knowing it." (Hebrews 13.2)

Restorative Justice Philosophy

Example I:

There was a man who stole some money and foodstuff from his neighbor. The neighbor, named Jacob, was bitter because he needed the money and food to feed his family. Jacob went to each neighbor on his floor asking if they knew anything about the theft. No one knew but each expressed their sympathy and offered whatever support they could give him. Jacob reported the theft to the police who recorded the pertinent data and promised to investigate.

Soon afterwards, John, Jacob's next door neighbor, suffered a similar fate but this time the suspect was seen by a resident while he was leaving John's apartment. The police were called and the suspect, Elwood, was apprehended. While in custody Elwood admitted to committing the two burglaries. He confessed that he needed the money and food to feed his family. He did not want to steal from others, but he had been unemployed for some time and was desperate. He saw no other way to resolve his problem.

Because Elwood was a first-time offender his case was referred to a community court, an adjudication process where community residents have an opportunity to determine the fate of those who engage in certain criminal behavior. Both John and Jacob were permitted to observe the process. The court discussed what was to be Elwood's punishment and how he might make amends. It was decided that Elwood would return the unspent money and unused food he had taken. During the proceedings it was learned that Elwood was an accomplished musician who at one time had taught music at the high school level. The neighborhood school had eliminated music and art from its curriculum due to budget reductions, so it was decided that Elwood would teach one music class for each grade once a week for two years. Parents who wished their child to take music would have to contribute five dollars a week for the course. Elwood would receive 75% of the proceeds. The remaining 25% would go toward repaying John and Jacob the balance of the money stolen from them. Once John and Jacob were repaid in full, Elwood would be allowed to keep 80% of the proceeds. The remaining 20% would be given to the court for expenses. To address Elwood's immediate family needs, the court referred him to appropriate social services and to religious agencies where he could obtain temporary assistance. Jacob, John and Elwood were satisfied with the court's ruling.[1]

Example II

A teenager named Janet stole some jewelry from a department store and traded the stolen items for drugs. She and some friends went to an abandoned building and got high. They became disorderly and began to break windows and damage the building.

The next day police investigated both crimes. They got a report from Mrs. Jones, the store manager, and they spoke with Mrs. Brown, a woman who lived next to the abandoned building. Mrs. Brown told the police that a group of girls had vandalized the building the day before and that she thought she recognized one of the girls from the neighborhood. She did not want to identify the suspect, though, for fear that the girl or members of her family might seek retribution. She also expressed concern that because the abandoned building was now in further disrepair, it would attract other groups of unruly youths. The police advised her to stay in her house and lock all of her windows and doors. They suggested that she inform her neighbors what had happened and urge them to take the same precautions. They reassured her that they would investigate the incidents thoroughly and, if they could, they would bring the guilty parties to justice.

The police were able to apprehend those involved in the incident. When they filed a report, the prosecutor felt they had enough evidence to try the case. A public defender was assigned to represent Janet. Her attorney negotiated a plea bargain and Janet was sentenced to a year of supervised probation, 200 hours of community service, and treatment for her substance abuse. She completed the requirements of her supervised probation, which included picking up paper in the public parks, and was discharged a year later.

Meanwhile, one year after the shoplifting incident, Mrs. Jones, the store manager, and Mrs. Brown, the neighbor, were unaware how the case had been resolved.

---

[1]Anne H. Crowe, "Restorative Justice and Offender Rehabilitation: A Meeting of the Minds," Annual Editions: *Criminal Justice* 1999/2000.

Janet had paid her debt to society through her community service work. She had become drug free by attending a substance abuse treatment program. She had even re-enrolled in college and was on her way to becoming a productive, law-abiding member of the community. Mrs. Jones had reported the theft of merchandise on her business income tax return, permitting her to contribute less in taxes to state and federal governments.

The abandoned building still had broken windows and increasing drug deals and drug use reportedly was taking place there. Mrs. Brown and her neighbors were afraid of the teenagers in the neighborhood and many of her neighbors have moved away, seeking a safer environment. Those who remained turned their homes into fortresses. Seldom did neighbors interact on the streets as they once had. The crime rate in the community increased during the last year.²

These stories illustrate two different responses to crime and punishment. One utilized what is today described as a *restorative philosophy*, focused on ensuring that the needs of all parties concerned – the victim, the offender, and the community – were taken into consideration when justice was rendered. The other, utilizing a *retributive* approach, focused primarily on the offender.

In today's climate of virtual anonymity, is it possible to respond to criminal wrongdoing in a manner that seeks to make those persons who commit criminal acts accountable for their behavior, while taking into account the interests and concerns of the victim and the community? Many believe it **is** possible and are working to demonstrate how it might be done. Of all the obstacles inherent in creating such a response, the greatest might very well hinge on the capacity to forgive and an ability to put a human face on those who are accused and found guilty of criminal behavior. This may be especially so when one realizes that a disproportionate number of people of color represent the bulk of the criminal justice system's clientele.

In ages past, restorative justice models could be found in many indigenous cultures. In pre-colonial New Zealand the Maori people had fully incorporated such a model in their legal processes. It was the traditional philosophy of Pacific nations such as Tonga, Fiji, and Samoa. "Restorative justice was the Pacific way."³ In pre-Norman Ireland, restorative justice was

---

²Crowe.
³Jim Consedine, *Restorative Justice: Healing the Effects of Crime* (Lyttelton, New Zealand: Ploughshares Publications, 1995).

successfully interwoven into the fabric of everyday life. With the absence of police, sheriffs or prisons, decisions of law were handled by the people involved "supported by a highly organized and disciplined public opinion springing from honor and interest and inherent in the solidarity of the clan."[4] The present-day restorative justice concept was developed in a Mennonite community in Canada in the 1970s. Restorative justice focuses primarily on people and not procedures. Crime is viewed as an offense against human relationships and only secondarily a violation of law. Therefore, in restorative justice the justice system should focus on healing those who have been hurt by the offense, both the victims and the perpetrators.[5]

Ron Classen, Co-Director of the Center for Peacemaking and Conflict Studies at Fresno Pacific College, describes restorative justice principles, in part, as recognizing that crime is wrong and should not occur but after it does, there are dangers and opportunities. The danger is that the community, victims and/or offender emerge from the response further alienated, more damaged, disrespected, dis-empowered, feeling less safe and less cooperative with society. The opportunity is that injustice is recognized, the equity is restored, and the future is clarified so participants are safer, more respectful and more empowered and cooperative with each other and society. Restorative justice is a process designed to make things as right as possible and includes attending to needs created by the offense, such as safety and repair of injuries, relationships and physical damage resulting from the offense. The process also attends to the needs related to the cause of the offense (addiction, lack of education, social or employment skills or resources).[6]

Classen asks, "Can there be an alternative to vengeance and retribution as a way of responding to a wrong or an injustice?" Walter Wink, in *Engaging the Powers: Discernment and Resistance in a World of Domination*, states that "our society's preferred response is one of vengeance." Wink has labeled this response "the myth of redemptive violence." He describes the myth of redemptive violence as "a belief that violence is an appropriate and necessary response, even healing for the victim, especially when administered by the

---

⁴Consedine.

⁵Robert D. Enright, "Community Forgiveness and Restorative Justice: Essays From the Criminal Justice System and the Peace Movement," *The International Institute, The World of Forgiveness* 2/4 (May 1999).

⁶Ron Classen, "Restorative Justice Principles Focus on People Not Procedures," *Victim-Offender Reconciliation Program Newsletter* (Fresno, California, 1996).

state on a victim's behalf."[7] Wink uses scripture to help us understand that there are alternatives to violence. In the fifth chapter of Matthew, Jesus says:

> You have heard that it was said, 'an eye for an eye.' But I say to you, offer no resistance to one who is evil. When someone strikes you on your right cheek, turn the other one to him as well. If one takes your tunic, give him your cloak as well. Should anyone press you into service for one mile, go with him for two miles.[8]

These statements may sound awfully weak and seem to call for the offended party to become a push-over. The average person will tune out because he knows that he does not have pleasant feelings for someone who has just committed a serious offense against him.

So how are we to understand and take seriously what Jesus is saying, when we have been offended? It appears that this is why Jesus immediately follows these statements with the command, "Love your enemy" (Mt 5: 44). Restorative justice should not be confused with approving, ignoring or saying that wrongdoing is okay. It has to involve assertive and constructive responses that bring appropriate attention to the problem in ways that encourage the offender to recognize and accept responsibility for the offense. To be effective, forgiveness and remorse will have to be integral components of the process. Although the impediments to forgiveness and remorse seem to be overwhelming, Professor Donald Goodman of John Jay College of Criminal Justice, an academic criminologist who has for several years administered conflict resolution and reconciliation programs in prisons, indicates that he senses new possibilities that the process of forgiveness is becoming another option in the criminal justice system.[9] He states:

> The basic posture of those accused by the state is to admit to as little as possible to avoid the threat of more severe sanctions. At many levels our police, courts and prisons are punishment driven with a primary focus on capture and sanction. They appear to leave little

---

[7]Walter Wink, *Engaging the Powers: Discernment and Resistance in a World of Domination* (Minneapolis: Fortress Press, 1992).

[8]Mt. 5: 38-41.

[9]Donald Goodman, *International Forgiveness Institute, The World of Forgiveness,* 2/4 (May 1999).

room for the development of forgiveness. So while there are safeguards to protect the innocent, a major goal and thrust of our massive criminal justice system is the identification, separation, and punishment of wrongdoers. Victims, who in most cases are left to heal their injuries and relieve their suffering as best they can on their own, find it difficult to forgive. In such an atmosphere, mistrust, suspicion and denial become magnified, hardened and institutionalized.[10]

Goodman asserts that exploring the option of forgiveness with citizens, victims, offenders and criminal justice practitioners could relieve our system's overriding bias toward punishment. Citizens could be helped to develop the necessary skills with respect to the forgiveness process prior to formal criminal justice proceedings. Practitioners could use elements of the forgiveness process to humanize the powerful forces of the criminal justice machinery. Goodman further states that "within our justice-seeking system, we must promote forgiveness not so much as an alternative, or a replacement, or a diminution of justice, but rather as an option that can help heal the grief and offer a path of reconnection for wrongdoers, victims and their community."[11]

Will we ever forget the awesome sight, with millions watching with us, of a smiling Nelson Mandela being released from a South African prison after serving twenty-seven years? Or the subsequent joy he and his fellow Black South Africans displayed when they voted for the first time and Mandela became president of the nation? What was most impressive was the message Mandela conveyed to the watching world by his actions and demeanor. After years of suffering under the brutality of a racist, unjust apartheid regime, his message was not one of vengeance or punishment but of restoration, healing, mercy and forgiveness.[12]

The families involved in the tragic murder of young Edward Werner in a New Jersey shore community have also demonstrated how forgiveness and reconciliation can facilitate the healing process. While selling candy door-to-door in September, 1997, eleven-year-old Ed Werner encountered Samuel Manzie, aged fifteen. It is reported that Samuel was despondent as a re-

---

[10]Goodman.
[11]Goodman.
[12]Consedine, 10.

sult of being involved with a 43-year-old convicted pedophile he met on the internet. Authorities have said that "Sam lured the boy into his home and strangled him with a necktie and a cord from a clock radio."[13] Samuel admitted to strangling the Werner boy in a fit of rage and power. At trial he pled guilty and was sentenced to a prison term of seventy years. The crime absorbed the community initially because of its brutality and again when it was learned that the Manzies had sought professional help for their son the month before the slaying. According to court records, they were unable to persuade the authorities that their son posed a danger.[14] Subsequent to the trial the Werner family filed a wrongful death lawsuit against the Manzies, the psychiatrists and the institutions that had been treating Samuel. The Manzies were shocked, and in return they contemplated filing a lawsuit of their own to protect themselves from potential damage awards. Two years later, with the help of Rev. Thomas P. Geoffroy, pastor of the Christian Life Fellowship Ministry, the two grief-stricken families decided to meet to begin what they hoped would be a healing process. "The time had come to start the healing," said Ed Werner, Sr., who asked pastor Geoffroy to contact Nicholas Manzie, Sam's father, to see if he would be willing to meet. "God was present at that meeting," Manzie said. "We just held each other. We couldn't hold each other tight enough. We wanted to make it OK." Reverend Geoffroy said, "Forgiveness is not a feeling but a decision. It will take a period of time to work and pray through forgiveness. There will still be times of painful emotions but this is a time of planting."[15]

The concept of restorative justice is being considered widely throughout the world. During a 1991 NATO-sponsored advanced research workshop in Italy, several countries, including the United States, presented papers on various aspects of restorative justice. While nations have different concerns and are moving at different speeds to implement restorative justice principles, they all are debating the shortcomings of a purely retributive system and the need for a more "holistic restorative philosophy."[16] Despite society's apparent preference for a retributive justice style, some areas of our justice system are experimenting with alternative ways of holding offenders accountable for their criminal behavior while ensuring that the needs and con-

---

[13]*Asbury Park Press*, Section A, page 1, September 27, 1999.
[14]*Asbury Park Press*, September 27, 1999.
[15]*Asbury Park Press*, September 27, 1999.
[16]*Asbury Park Press*, September 28, 1999, Section A, page 1.

cerns of the victim and the community are addressed. Will our system ever be able to embrace, in a meaningful way, restorative justice as a viable response option to crime? Do we have the will to become a truly civilized society?

Responses to Crime

America is a violent culture where many violent acts are perpetrated against individuals. The state, in turn, often uses violent measures to apprehend and punish offenders. Anyone familiar with our penitentiary system will know that being incarcerated is anything but a rehabilitating experience. Some believe that the penitentiary's focus changed from rehabilitation to punishment when its clientele changed from white to black and Latino.

All of us have been concerned about or affected by crime. Many of us have either been a victim or know someone who has been victimized. We may even know someone who has committed a crime. Media reports remind us of the most recent local, national or international crime incidents. We agonize after hearing of the latest homicide, bombing, robbery, rape, hate crime, sexual molestation or domestic violence incident. We cannot escape the fear or anxiety that crime engenders. However, we should realize that although acts of violent crime have been reduced, the current crimes for which many offenders are incarcerated are minor, non-violent in nature.

According to the Correctional Association of New York, the 1973 Rockefeller drug law which requires harsh prison terms for possession or sale of relatively small amounts of drugs is responsible for filling our prison with low-level, non-violent offenders, at a great expense to the taxpayer. In New York State 22,300 drug offenders are incarcerated at a cost of more than $710,000,000.[17] In 1997, 44.5% of those persons sent to prison were drug offenders. In 1980, the figure was 11%. Over 25% of the drug offenders incarcerated in New York prisons, nearly 6,000 people, were locked up for drug *possession*, not drug sales. It cost about $190,000,000 to keep these people in prison annually. Nearly 60% of the drug offenders in New York State prisons were convicted of the three lowest felonies-Class C, D or E-

---

[17] The Correctional Association of New York, "Juvenile Detention in New York City Report," (February, 2000), 1.

which involve only minute drug amounts.[18] Only ten percent of the inmates in New York State have a high school equivalency diploma. Seventy-five percent of the prisoners do not have a high school diploma. An estimated 40% cannot read. A high percentage have learning disabilities, come from poverty neighborhoods that are served by the worst schools, and are products of dysfunctional families.[19]

Regretfully, many citizens of color are disproportionately involved with and impacted by crime. Studies conducted by The Community Justice Center of New York City, an inmate advocacy organization, indicate that the majority of inmates incarcerated in the state of New York come from fewer than eighteen zip codes. These neighborhoods serve as a feeder system for the prison-industrial complex. In light of this information, it seems that our society would benefit more by allocating resources and human services to these neighborhoods instead of spending the $100,000 per cell it costs to build new prisons. What is it that prevents us from understanding and empathizing with the plight of those who struggle to survive in these communities? Why do we seem unaffected by or unwilling to stem this flow of humanity into what for most will be a dehumanizing, dead-end system?

The story of Francis and the wolf of Gubbio can serve as an example of how we might respond to our crime problem. The people of Gubbio had been terrorized by and were fearful of the wolf. They knew little about the wolf except that he was hungry and was eating their livestock; even some townspeople had perished. Because of their fear of the wolf they were unable to resolve the conflict between the wolf and the town. Francis, upon visiting the town and learning of the situation, decided he would try to help the people of Gubbio. Against the warning of the townspeople he left the security of the village and reached out to the wolf, secure in the belief that his faith would protect him. Francis was able to reconcile the differences between the wolf and townspeople by getting the wolf to promise not to terrorize the town and getting the townspeople to promise to pay closer attention to the wolf's needs.[20] I see the wolf as a metaphor for the criminal element, the "other," in our society. They terrorize us because we fail to be concerned about their needs. Like Francis, we are challenged to reach out in

---

[18]Scott Christianson, *Balancing Justice in New York State: A Citizen's Fact Book* (League of Women Voters of New York State: 1999), 38.

[19]*Balancing Justice*, 37.

[20] See any version of *The Little Flowers of St. Francis*.

faith to seek to resolve the conflicts that exist between those whose criminal behavior terrorizes us by and their victims, as well as between the perpetrators and the larger community and the state.

During the late 1980s and early 1990s, our nation's approach to crime changed dramatically. Due to a perception that criminal behavior was increasing and miscreants were not being sufficiently contained and punished, society stiffened its attitude toward criminal offenders. Police professionals, believing that they could prevent crime instead of just react to it, instituted a more aggressive policing style. This new proactive mind-set was stimulated, in part, by the introduction of new theories, strategies and practices such as "Broken Windows," community policing and Compstat (computerized statistics).

The Broken Window theory, fashioned by George Kelling and James Q. Wilson in 1981, encourages law enforcement to devote more attention to quality of life crimes, those minor crimes-graffiti, panhandling, public urination, subway fare-beating, disorderly conduct, public consumption of alcohol or beer or smoking marijuana-that are thought to be the precursors to serious crime. Order maintenance in public space became a priority.[21]

The Compstat model (computerized statistics), instituted at the New York City Police Department in 1994 by former Police Commissioner William Bratton and his deputy Jack Maple, is designed to utilize crime statistics when analyzing and planning responses to criminal incidents. An important aspect of Compstat is that precinct commanders are held accountable for crime-reduction strategies and results within their commands. While the use of Compstat has proven to be beneficial to law enforcement, incorporating into police work the latest management practices and technology tools, some believe that a negative by-product has emerged. As a primarily data-driven process, Compstat has been accused of placing pressure on precinct commanders to produce desirable numbers. In turn, the patrol officer is pressured by his commander to produce. In this pressurized atmosphere, some think the new policing mind-set has become, particularly in New York City, a numbers game-how many arrests have been made, how many guns have been confiscated, how many DWI motor vehicles have been im-

---

[21]George L. Kelling and James Q. Wilson, "Broken Windows: the Police and Neighborhood Safety," *The Atlantic Monthly* (March, 1982):29-38.

pounded? Such a posture has caused an uncomfortable relationship between the police and some communities they serve.

During the early 1990s, the use of Community Policing strategies (a process involving police agencies and communities working in partnership in an effort to reduce crime and maintain public safety) has proven to be an effective tool in several jurisdictions. The process enables police and residents to develop meaningful relationships by fostering a better understanding of each other's needs. Utilizing a collaborative problem solving strategy, the police and community residents engage in identifying and eliminating the causes of crime. Ideally, once the causes of crime have been targeted, the resources of the city, state or municipality will be directed to eradicating the problem. Some jurisdictions have embraced the Community Policing model more readily than others. New York City has stressed a tough, aggressive style of enforcement that has caused the deterioration of police-community relations in communities of color. Other cities, however, have shown that police-community collaboration can effectively reduce crime and improve relations, especially in communities of color, without having to utilize a rough-and-tumble approach.

San Diego and Boston, for example, have managed to reduce crime by using several variations of the community policing model without further exacerbating relations between the police and the citizenry. The Boston Police Department has been able to partner with black clergy and other community-based organizations to lower crime significantly, reduce gang violence, and remove illegal handguns from the streets. Between 1991 and 1998, they reduced the homicide rate by 69.3% and the robbery rate by 50.2%. San Diego, realizing that its police force was not large enough to effectively do all that was necessary to combat crime, encouraged the participation of residents to help in the effort. During the period between 1991 and 1998, San Diego led all American cities in reducing homicides by 76.4% and robbery by 62.6%.[22]

In the last decade politicians and legislators, responding to the perceived wishes of their constituents, began pressuring a judiciary system that heretofore seemed reluctant to prosecute for minor crimes. Tougher and mandatory sentences were urged. "Three strikes and you're out policies" were

---

[22]Fox Butterfield, "Cities Reduce Crime and Conflict Without New York Style Hardball." *The New York Times*, March 4, 2000, pp. A1 and B4.

enacted in some jurisdictions. The results have been a ballooning incarceration rate. In 1999, nearly two million persons were imprisoned in the United States.[23] Although crimes in all major categories have been reduced, the number of persons incarcerated continues to increase. Juveniles accused of committing serious crimes can now be prosecuted as adults. Courts are scrupulously *not* sentencing offenders to probation. The elimination of parole and less rehabilitative and recreational services for inmates has become the norm because of the probability of repeat offenders and the sentiment that the penitentiary is suppose to be punishment. These and other measures have combined to send a message that criminal behavior will not be tolerated and criminals will no longer be coddled.

In creating new or refined strategies, special undercover units were formed to target particular patterns of offenses. For example, in New York City, a Street Crimes Unit (SCU), a specially-trained plainclothes unit that was first created in 1971 as part of the Anti-Crime Section, is charged with the responsibility of removing illegal handguns from city streets. While this unit has been successful in confiscating many illegal guns by using the "stop and frisk" tactic, it has also been accused of violating the civil liberties of many law-abiding citizens. As a result of the SCU's aggressive "stop and frisk" tactics that primarily targeted people of color, numerous accusations of racial profiling (the singling out of persons based solely on race or color), have exacerbated an already-strained relationship between the police and communities of color. It is interesting that data provided by the NYPD on its "stop and frisk" activity indicates that while 1 in 9.5 stops of blacks resulted in arrests, when whites were stopped the arrest result was 1 in 7.9.[24] This suggests that if whites were subjected to the kind of intense scrutiny and surveillance that people of color are subjected to, their arrest-and-conviction rate might exceed the rates recorded for people of color.

The killing of Amadou Diallo, a West African immigrant in the Bronx, NY, by four white members of the SCU on February 4, 1991, focused national and international attention on the pattern and practices of the NYPD, particularly as the department relates to the policing of communities of color. In numerous instances, white police officers have found it necessary to use deadly force against black and Latino unarmed civilians. Critics point to

---

[23]Bureau of Justice Statistics (2000), 19.
[24]*The New York City Police Department's "Stop & Frisk" Practices: A Report To the People of The State of New York from the Office of The Attorney General* (1999), 111.

police culture and the perceptions and attitudes of white officers toward people of color as reasons why excessive and deadly force is sometimes used. However, while race might be a factor in these incidents, it must be noted that black and brown officers have also been involved in situations where excessive, deadly force was used against persons of color. Clearly, explaining the inappropriate use of deadly force is more complicated than just ascribing it to racial issues. Other factors are at play – including fear, misperception, an abuse of power, and persons hired to be police officers who may not be suited for the job.

Police work in a free, democratic society requires that an officer be mature, intelligent, psychologically and emotionally balanced, skilled in human relations, and a culturally competent professional. Culturally competent is to be understood in the sense that he/she has the capacity to effectively interact in a pluralistic, culturally diverse society. The SCU's motto of "We own the night" or the Hemingway quote, "There is no hunting like the hunting of man and those who have hunted armed men long enough and liked it, never really care for anything else thereafter,"[25] is not the kind of philosophy the public believes its police should adopt. Certainly not all police officers subscribe to these sentiments. But it is clear that some do.

Building Communities of Faith

Several Franciscan ministries exist that advocate for and serve those who are at risk of becoming drawn into the criminal justice system or who have already been snared in the system. In 1968, Father Benedict Taylor, O.F.M., and a team of Franciscans went to Harlem, New York, to witness among those who suffered from drug abuse and addiction. This witness resulted in the establishment of Project Create, Inc., which evolved over time into a multi-service ministry that provides spiritual guidance, drug treatment, psychological health care, housing, education, and job training for youth and adult males, the majority of whom were of African-American or Latino ancestry.

Father Ben, as he is affectionately known, realized that adequate drug treatment services were not available for this particular population and that

---

[25]Ernest Hemingway, "On the Blue Water: A Gulf Stream Letter," *Esquire* (April, 1936). Reprinted in *By-line: Ernest Hemingway, Selected Articles and Dispatches of Four Deacdes*, ed. William White (NY: Simon and Schuster, 1981) 236.

most of the individuals who had a drug problem were finding their way into the criminal justice system. Many who were suffering from drug abuse knew that, basically, the only way they would be able to receive treatment for their problem was to be incarcerated.

Drug laws in New York State have disproportionately affected communities of color. Thirty-two percent of young men of African descent aged 20-29 are under some form of criminal justice supervision-incarceration, probation or parole.[26] African-Americans comprise almost 50% of the state prison population while they represent only 12.4% of the state's total population. Latinos make up 33% of the inmate population while constituting only 10.8% of the overall state's population.[27] It seems clear that law enforcement has targeted inner city neighborhoods for drug enforcement, despite the fact that most drug consumption or sale does not occur there. Studies have shown that the vast majority of people who deal in and consume illegal drugs are of European ancestry (White). Yet, the overwhelming majority of inmates in New York State prisons for drug arrests are Black and Latino. Moreover, the January, 1999, report from the Citizens' Committee for Children of New York titled: "Myth and Realities of the Juvenile Justice System" stated that although arrests for violent juvenile crime has decreased in New York by 28% since 1994, the number of youths being placed in detention facilities is higher than it has been this entire decade.[28]

Believing that it should not be necessary for someone with a drug problem to go to prison in order to receive treatment, Fr. Ben would visit criminal courts and petition judges to release offenders with drug problems into his supervision. Once in his care, these individuals would receive the kind of personal attention and assistance that allowed them to embark on a rehabilitation journey; eventually their rehabilitation would lead to independent living by obtaining and holding meaningful employment.

In 1970, Create, Inc., with $500.00 that was provided by Saint Francis Church on West 31st Street, New York City, purchased its first building at 121-123 West 111th Street. Create formally began its residential drug-free treatment services at this location in 1973. Men in the Create program were

---

[26]Marc Maurer and Tracy Huling, *Young Black Americans and The Criminal Justice System: Five Years Later, The Sentencing Project* (October, 1995), 1.

[27]*The HUB System:: Profiles of Inmates under Custody on January 1, 1999* (State of New York Department of Correctional Services), 7.

[28]"Keeping Track of New York City's Children," *The Citizens Committee for Children Report*, 1999.

given an opportunity to learn various building trades by performing much of the carpentry, electrical, masonry, and plumbing work that the building needed.

In 1976, Create, Inc. purchased its second building at 128 West 111th Street, for $25.000.00. This site became *Create House*, a shelter for homeless men. Subsequent growth has led to the establishment of a youth adult center, a senior program, a housing and supportive services program for single persons and single parents with children, and a food pantry.[29] Fr. Ben says that while it requires certain human relations and administration skills to successfully minister with persons who have drug problems, what is most required is a desire to help. There is a unique reward in helping those who are considered in the minds of some people to be the "dross of society" to improve their lives and become productive members of the community.

Since 1972 the Cephas-Attica Program has ministered to help meet the needs of men and women in prison and on parole. The ministry is located at two sites, St. Patrick's Friary in Buffalo, New York, and in Rochester, New York. The program's goals are to enrich the quality of life of each individual it serves by helping him or her to gain a deeper self-awareness. The offender is encouraged to accept personal responsibility for his or her life and actions; to achieve a spiritual reawakening; and to develop a true desire to change his/her life style and be healed. Clients are helped to take whatever steps are necessary for change to happen in order to become a productive member of society. Franciscan friars and volunteers visit offenders in several prisons throughout New York State, conduct group discussions with inmates and parolees to help them understand how their behavior resulted in their being incarcerated, and assist in the offender's transition back into the community. Temporary housing is also available as well as job and work-ethic training. Brother Michael Oberst, Coordinator of the Buffalo branch, explains:

> " . . . these men and women are not coming from a nine-to-five lunch box background. Most have no idea how to look for work, how to meet problems or make choices as they arise, how to become normalized. They need to be taught these skills so that when the same problems they had previously, the same bad friends or bad

---

[29]Create, Inc. literature.

habits crop up, they will be able to say, "No, this isn't the way to solve this."[30]

Since its beginning, Cephas has expanded enormously but, sadly, so has the need. When the program began in 1972 shortly after the Attica riot, New York State had 21 prisons and 12,400 inmates. Today there are more than 50,000 inmates being housed in 55 institutions. Prison overcrowding is a problem. Yet, despite its lack of sufficient resources, the Cephas recidivism rate of 15-20% is low compared to the estimated 60% rate of those who do not participate in the program.

The annual cost to house an inmate in New York State is about $26,000. In 1999, 102 Cephas visitors made 1,370 prison visits. Over four thousand (4647) inmates attended Cephas group sessions.[31] The help Cephas is providing costs a lot less than what the state pays to house an inmate. For a civilized society, the program's results of helping offenders to become productive citizens should be viewed as a more desirable objective than spending enormous sums of tax-payer money on prison construction and operations. Often, men and women who commit crime do so because they are unable to meet life's everyday challenges and obstacles. Through his involvement with the Cephas ministry, Brother Michael has discovered that "it is a privilege to live with and serve the poor-those who can't manage their own lives. I've found Christ among them."[32]

These are two examples of Franciscans ministering in the criminal justice arena. Others are in the vineyard. More are needed to bring change to a complex bureaucracy that dehumanizes millions who are caught in its web. "The harvest in plentiful, but the workers are few."

---

[30]*The Anthonian*, February, 1990.
[31]Cephas 1999 Annual Report.
[32]Cephas 1999 Annual Report.

Conclusion

As we enter the third century of Christianity, much remains to be done to meet the challenge of building a community inclusive of those who have been marginalized because of their criminal behavior. We are challenged to build bridges of healing, forgiveness, and reconciliation between victim and offender and between the offender, the community and the state. It is also necessary to develop an improved level of understanding between the community and those who are sworn to protect and serve. To achieve these goals, addressing the concerns of the offenders and the causes of crime, is crucial. In this regard, I am reminded of Charles Dutton's life story and believe that his story may very well resemble the story of lots of people who commit crime.

Charles Dutton, nicknamed ROC because of the tough reputation he earned on the mean streets of Baltimore, is a stage, screen and television star who, as a youth, killed a man in a bar fight. As a result, he was imprisoned for eight years. While incarcerated, Dutton became interested in the theater and acting. He read all he could about these subjects and participated in plays that were staged at the prison. August Wilson, the acclaimed playwright and director of the Yale University Repertory Theater, heard of Dutton's interest and work and invited him to attend Yale upon his release. Once discharged, Dutton headed straight for New Haven. Under Wilson's tutelage Dutton honed his craft. Wilson wrote a play, *The Piano Lesson*, expressly for Dutton. When it came to Broadway with Dutton in the leading role, it was a smash hit. Dutton became a star. While the play was enjoying a successful run on Broadway, Dutton was interviewed on television's *60 Minutes*. During the conversation he was asked if he ever felt remorse for the life he had taken. He initially paused, seemingly surprised by the question, but then answered, "No, not at first." He stated that he did not begin to feel remorse for his victim or the victim's family until his own life had meaning.

In the spirit of Francis the peacemaker, let us pray that we will have the commitment and courage to transform our justice system into one that focuses on restoration instead of retribution. A system that will assist with repairing and healing the damage done to victims and the community, and one that will increase our capacity to forgive. Such a system would attempt to eliminate the causes of crime and give meaning to the lives of potential offenders. There are specific ways to effectively redirect the lives of those who are at risk of committing criminal acts: they will need to be accepted by, be-long to, and count for something meaningful in, society. It is doubtful that we will arrest our way out of the crime problem.

Herbert Johnson is the Associate Director of the Criminal Justice Center at John Jay College of Criminal Justice/CUNY. His areas of interest are school safety, workplace violence, human relations and cultural diversity training.

Questions for Reflection

1. In your ministry how do you challenge retributive justice?

2. Are there new ways to redefine the crime and punishment debate in America?

3. What strategies can religious leaders use to influence public policy regarding crime and justice?

Francis of Assisi and the Strengths Perspective: Guiding Principles for Franciscan Urban Ministries

William Margraf, M.S.W.

Introduction: Social Analysis

The context of urban ministry is born of social imbalances and injustices found in concentrated areas of densely multicultural populations. Situations faced by society as a whole are magnified immensely in any given urban area. The call to serve the people of these conditions and circumstances is not new, and the minister will always find abundant work. The tools and skills a minister employs are many and diverse. Franciscan ministry, as in the case of many other ministries, may use sociological assessments, community organizing, social services outreach, and ecclesial and socioeconomic networks to facilitate some change in the environments in which they serve. The goals are often the similar: rooted in the Gospel, a mode of service is developed to enhance the well-being of the socially marginalized.

The plight of the immigrant, the continually scarring effect of racism, the alienation of the socially undesirable and dispossessed, and community-starved people are the focus of urban ministry. What the urban minister can construct in terms of programs, networks, and community organizing is critical to the improvement of desperate lives seemingly trapped in a cycle of poverty and injustice. This chapter will endeavor not to analyze what urban ministries do, rather it will hope to elucidate a particular way in which the Franciscan religious or layperson may minister in the urban context. After an examination of some of Francis' own ministerial principles and their applications, an overview of a theoretical system of social work/social service thought will be introduced to contextualize Franciscan approaches in a structured church or agency model of service. While obviously Franciscan ministerial principles stand on their own merit, the thrust of this article is to assist urban ministries begin or re-imagine their work by understanding more deeply the critical disposition of the basic relationship between the minister and the person or population served. The ministry Francis of Assisi offered is rooted in a sense of justice and right relationship among God, the one who serves and the one served. Such a tradition still holds great significance and offers impetus for contemporary ministry.

Francis and an Interpretation of His Ministry

In identifying himself as a minister of the Gospel of Jesus Christ, Francis undertook various roles in his conception of service in the name of God. Among these roles three stand out in discerning the model of service for Franciscans in urban ministry: healer, peacemaker, and community builder. In all three ministerial dispositions Francis was singularly focused on building the Kingdom. The intrinsic element of his work was that of enabling authentic, mutual, renewed and healed relationships. The strength of this venture lay in his certainty of God's presence in bringing about new possibilities relationally which had suffered or had been fractured by the pressures of a world in transition, despair, conflict or isolation. Francis saw a world of potential and promise. His life in ministry might be interpreted as a process of healing through the identification of both creation's strengths and the created's needs, all rooted in the Creator's love. This counter-cultural focus still challenges society's subtle and often virulent disregard in its drive to divide and scapegoat the perceived weak and alien. Francis in his own identification with poverty was able to construct an approach to loving the Supreme and all-merciful Creator through every aspect of life. Every part of creation was the source of praise for him as he dismantled the limits the world had placed on the poor, the alienated and the marginalized.

The Leper and Francis: Mutual Healing

As Francis was coming to terms with what his new life with God might entail, his encounter with the leper on the roadside served as a defining moment in his spiritual journey. This experience with the poor, forgotten and diseased man helped Francis begin to grasp the lived realities of poverty and acceptance. While poverty can be lived without acceptance, the saint of Assisi came to understand that the integration of the two was critical in following the Gospel life. In poverty one can identify further with the poor Christ and those who are socially marginalized and alienated. By eschewing the trappings of power and privilege, as well as convenience and contentment, Francis took on a newfound meaning of the Incarnation. Rejecting worldly accouterment facilitated his ministry of service to the poor as a poor man himself. To be without all which had been impressed upon him as necessary for the good life and to embrace a life contingent on the assistance of others was fundamental to Francis' reflection of Christ. And yet it is apparent in the story of the leper that a sense of poverty means not only going without material wealth. Further to the point of the lesson of the leper is Francis' realization that in actualizing the Gospel life there was an essential interdependence between him and the leper. The leper's needs for physical attention to his diseased body as well as his emotional needs for companionship are met in Francis' surprising response of offering comfort and even validation. Similarly, the leper is able to bring Francis to a deeper understanding of the Gospel. It is here that Francis needs the leper to overcome his own spiritual isolation so as to move more deeply in the experience of the ennobling and fully inclusive Christ. The whole encounter serves as an illustration of the interdependence of the minister and the poor. What is not clear in this story is which person is playing which role.

The leper and Francis help the saint's heirs to consider the role of poverty in the ministerial relationship. On the roadside there is clearly a constructive motivation for Francis to serve one he has identified as worthy of service. And yet it is the leper who grants permission to receive the Poverello's ministrations. The dynamic of power is therefore upended in the normative sense. Inasmuch, the two are playing two roles equally: one cannot effectively minister without the other also providing a similar service. Poverty, therefore, takes on a new, shared and even paradoxical meaning in that Francis came to practice ministry as an interdependent way of being and serving. What began as an act of charity to temporarily ameliorate a poor man's condition became an encounter of mutuality leading to a wealth of shared service and spiritual insight.

The Wolf and the Community of Gubbio: Peacemaking

Another illustration of Francis' ministry is found in the story of the wolf of Gubbio. Resisting the warnings of fearful villagers of Gubbio, Francis stalked off to what might be anticipated as a life-threatening confrontation of the wolf terrorizing the town. Yet, the little poor one moved toward the wolf without the emotional frenzy of fear and hysteria which gripped the townspeople. He could not begin a ministerial relationship with the wolf if he had subjected himself to the bias and the fear of the populace he served on this occasion. The freedom from bias in this situation led him to the possibility of meeting a social need through the spirit, a service which could not come from the social context of Gubbio. He entered the meeting with the wolf by being freed of others' perception of this terror, being poor enough so as not to emotionally "buy into" or succumb to the hysteria, and being singular in approaching it with only the sign of the Cross (the symbol of co-suffering, trust, acceptance and conversion). Francis was able to begin a three-fold process: a process of peace between the feared and the fearful, a process of acceptance of the other, and a process of conversion for both the community and the outcast.

Francis was quickly able to get at the cause of the wolf's behavior. It may be seen in the simple approach he took toward the wolf which perhaps made the most significant impact. While the wolf could have lunged at Francis, the little poor one did not demonstrate any fear or bravado, actions which would have fueled the violence further. Rather, he continued to move toward the wolf with a simple demonstration of faith and trust. At that moment the wolf's isolation was broken and, to the animal's probable surprise, a relationship ensued. It might be said Francis had daring or chutzpah, but more certainly he had faith in the possibility of relating to this threat to Gubbio. Francis' faith extended beyond mere piety; it was maintaining faith in the face of fear which facilitated a ministerial breakthrough (and, ultimately, appeasement for all involved). With Francis' mediation this ministerial action created a new perspective of the wolf by making known its needs, its hurt and its subsequent willingness to change because of the safety and inclusion newly provided by the citizens of Gubbio.

Ever being a person of balance and symmetry, Francis crafted an arrangement which met the needs of both the wolf and the Gubbians. Francis facilitated an understanding through dialogue between the previously estranged parties where all could live peacefully and, eventually, in joy and thanksgiving. While the wolf and the town made peace for their respective and mutual benefit, Francis inserted himself as the bondsman, the one whom the people could sue if the wolf broke his end of the bargain. This appears to be a safeguard for the wolf's well-being whose fragility in being accepted and cooperative was tenuous considering his status as poor, hungry, and alienated. Similarly, Francis perhaps was taking on the burden of sin of the villagers for their lack of compassion for the wolf while protecting the wolf from the possible re-emergence of his learned reactions to society's hostile treatment of him. Francis places himself at both risk and as the keystone of peace. If the arrangement had been somehow threatened or broken, Francis would have had to answer for it, or more certainly pay for it. Considering his own poverty this was a circumstance he could not afford, literally or figuratively. His faith and trust in the spirit working through people and the wolf was the only asset he had. Thus, his full reliance on the people, the wolf and the intervention of the Holy Spirit were the simple and only tools the little poor one needed in effecting peace, ending violence, overcoming fear, and meeting the needs of others.

The Canticle of Brother Sun: Community Building

In the *Canticle of Creation* Francis sets forth an understanding of the interrelationships between all parts of the created world as gifts from God who in turn have their one meaning in being of praise for the Father. Francis' perspective elucidates the constructive qualities of each facet of nature as the keys to creation's collective goal of being harmonized so as to reflect God's love for them individually and as a whole. The metaphor of many parts forming a synergistic unity may be seen as the result of Francis' grasp of the Eucharist. By taking the sun, moon, earth, fire, water, and even death and interpersonal relations as simple forms of creation and then offering them in thanksgiving to the Creator he consecrates the natural order as blessed elements holy and good. It is in the disposition of the acceptance of God's munificence for the world through others that Francis is able to forge a universal communion with the Father.

The concepts of personalism, mutuality and community may be three of the many concepts which underscore the *Canticle* as a model of ministry. The value of each part mentioned in the poem-prayer is held up for its own goodness. Each created element (the sun, moon, etc.) is identified as a "person," and therefore seen as intrinsically blessed and full of purpose. The role of each element is essential and meaningful to the other elements. While each is uniquely dignified, it is their unity which brings them all to fulfillment in the Creator. Their respective dignity is celebrated for what it is in itself and for what it is in relation to God. The order described by Francis seems to understand the inherent need for each element to be recognized, respected and given responsibility to participate in the dynamic of the whole.

That Francis was able to imagine the possibility of calling all of nature to its highest degree of realization is remarkable. His being was able to metaphorically unify all elements through the spirit into a single voice is nothing short of an immense grasp of the meaning of the kingdom of God. And yet, Francis' poetry was not formed out of some idealistic inexperience; rather it emerged from his own identification with the Crucified Christ. Through his ministry, and his sacrifice and suffering, Francis' spiritual quest led him to know the impact of the difficulty and dissolution of personal and community relationships. He observed the world and deeply felt for those who were castigated for their limitations and diseases, whether they were physical, emotional, social, or spiritual. Perhaps Francis understood the ruinous result of a fractured, wounded world and its propensity to turn inward and upon itself as a reaction to continually inflicted abuse. Like Christ, the saint of Assisi had not only observed the pain and degradation of the poor but shared in it with empathy so deep that his only action was to humbly offer it to the Father so as for it to be transformed.

Francis, the Healing Relationship and its Contemporary Applications

The urban dynamic reflects the panoply of nearly all human conditions. The varied and diverse lives encountered by the Franciscan minister pose unique and very often overwhelming challenges. Francis himself seems to have been open to all who sought his evangelical attention. The concern he shared with each person whom he encountered was on some level a transformative experience in itself. The charism exuded by Francis was uniquely his own. His power to make significant even the most socially reprehensible character has become one of Francis' most widely admired traits. The implications of this ministerial approach for the Franciscan minister offer a unique and occasionally unconventional manner of enlivening the Gospel through the medium of the human relationship.

Whether it was with the leper or the wolf or in his grasp of the interconnection of the elements of the universe, Francis' "success" was to be found in the essence of relationship. His identification with the varied parts of the creation served as a backdrop to the intimacy he helped to nurture between himself and the other, human or otherwise, all within the loving presence of God. Perhaps because of his belief in this purpose and the constructive role each created being played in the whole of the world, Francis could only play out his part by facilitating relationship to further effect the building of the Kingdom. While his message was clearly spoken in terms of the Good News, it might be necessary to consider how deeply his disposition, his availability and even his physical form and gestures extended the saving call to those to whom he preached, served and shared life. His insight into the value of relationship as a subtle yet critical key to the will of God may have been meaningless in terms of the "effective work" of ministry, but it surely was a most complete response to the call of all received in baptism.

The examination of both the role of minister and social service provider in a Franciscan-oriented agency (as well as the operation of the agency itself) will be considered at this point. The two levels of work (the micro- and macro-level) within such a setting will be explored in terms of both the philosophical understanding of social work as well as the Franciscan ministerial meaning from which such work is based and can be further cultivated. The role of the Franciscan social service provider affords the operative realization of constructive and goal-focused ministry. It is hoped the description of the two following concepts of the therapeutic alliance and non-possessive warmth will augment or offer greater structure to a given ministry site as well as fostering a dynamic expression of the Franciscan charism.

The translation from the saintly manner of Francis (in relating to all creation) to the most mundane of ministerial action of our own lives may be an impossible task. Yet, even at the most basic level, each person has at least some capacity to form and maintain relationships. Francis might be for us the most easily identifiable person with the gift of cultivating deep and God-centered relationships. While his particular gift may be unique to him, so it is for each person to nurture constructive and generous relationships, given the opportunity. For Francis the power of relationships has infinite possibilities when realized within the Spirit. The Franciscan minister (lay or religious) bears the yoke of this tradition to perpetuate a certain openness in relating that encourages creativity within the parameters of ministerial relationships.

Hope and Healing: The Therapeutic Alliance

If the three concepts of Franciscan ministry (healing, peacemaking, and community-building) are to be practiced with efficacy in a social service environment, an understanding of the various vehicles for such an endeavor is necessary. For Francis' spiritual and ministerial heirs, a response focused on the contemporary realities of the urban life is in need of greater development in terms of the value of relationship between the minister and to those "receiving" ministry. For ministers in the field of social service and social work a bridge between the Franciscan tradition and professional standards is essential in the attempt to heal and re-build the urban environment. A parallel of the Franciscan ministerial context can be found in the professional stance of social work.

The "therapeutic alliance" serves as the cornerstone of any healing process attempted by the social worker and the client. The qualities of the therapeutic alliance include empathy, respect, non-possessive warmth, and authenticity (or genuineness). It may be seen that Francis intuitively reflected these values in his ministry. This point does not make Francis a social worker, nor will it make a social worker "Franciscan." But in the development of those who practice social work or provide some kind of social service within the framework of a Franciscan ministry, it may be valuable to make the connection of how it is possible to integrate the traditional Franciscan ministerial approach with otherwise secularized professional standards.

The spirit of collaboration is recognized in the therapeutic alliance to the extent that it contributes to the process of addressing a need or concern by the "client." As the client or population enters the initial engagement process, the agency or social worker/service provider will draw on the reflection and practice experience of how to express respect and empathy to the client or population. This early step in the therapeutic alliance is critical in inculcating trust to spark collaboration. Collaboration facilitates both the mutuality and the equality necessary for an authentic relationship. Trust is therefore grounded when the partnership is established in terms of accountability and a sense of constructive and meaningful response between the minister/provider and the faithful/client as in the story of the wolf of Gubbio. This is also reflective of the way Francis defined the workings of creation in *The Canticle of Creation:* a cooperative and mutually appreciative dynamic at work for the personal and communal good of all involved. This alliance or relationship offers an immediate and realistic context to practice Franciscan ministry in the concrete application of social services. It forms a genuine expression of solidarity with those with whom ministry is shared.

Non-possessive warmth is a term used to describe the social worker's expression of care and concern for the client without any will to control or manipulate, while empathy is seen as the understanding another person's feelings and circumstances without necessarily voicing or feeling agreement.[1] Non-possessive warmth does not connote friendship or a friendly attachment; rather, it speaks to the worthiness of attention and service offered by Christ and Francis. It essentially deems the "other" in the ministerial or professional relationship as significant and necessary in salvific and therapeutic terms. This "joining" process speaks to the respect and dignity inherent in the therapeutic alliance. In his ministry to the leper and the wolf Francis employed each of these qualities, not in a therapeutic setting but as a moment of healing through gentle awareness and identification with them.

For the Franciscan minister the question always remains: to what end does my action serve? The implications of each of Francis' ministerial forays were not solely for the amelioration of a condition or conflict in and of itself. Rather, Francis knew through his relational approach the Kingdom's realization would be a bit more at hand. Similarly, the social worker/social service provider in a Franciscan agency may have several "tracks" of thought in any mode of work. First, how is it possible to realize with the client or population a sense of mutual understanding and trust? Second, how is the "backdrop" of this Franciscan agency and this client or population identifying itself collectively as subscribing to a spirit of unity and cooperation as a force from which greater circumstances are possible? And lastly, in reflecting on the meaning of "non-possessive," how does this synergistic entity (the agency with the clients) work through dependence and interdependence issues in its realization of it goals, and beyond?

The therapeutic alliance and non-possessive warmth may be seen as concrete ways in which ministry is practiced, especially in the realization of social services in a Franciscan-oriented setting. Hopefully, it may be practiced so as to embody the three cardinal principles of Catholic social justice:

---

[1]Dean H. Hepworth and Jo Ann Larson, *Direct Social Work Practice: Theory and Skills, Fourth Edition* (Pacific Grove, CA: Brooks/Cole, 1993), 55-56.

personalism, subsidiarity and pluralism. The further application of these principles can be found in a more pervasive utilization called the strengths perspective.

The Strengths Perspective

As previously discussed, Francis' approach to ministry was singularly and deeply rooted in his relationship with God. The identity he developed from this relationship and the work he accomplished was based on a shared life with the loving and almighty One. Out of his option for poverty he saw opportunity; from his counter-cultural perspective he perceived the possibility of a life vastly more rich than could be obtained materially. In his age the unique path of Francis must have been baffling for his contemporaries, and yet the essence of the Franciscan charism was distilled and perpetuated despite its challenge to the mainstream. The manner in which Francis ministered offered to the poor affirmation of their significance in the Kingdom of God. The function of ministry is not merely to attend to the poor; it is in the process of strengthening, imagining, and encouraging those identified as brothers and sisters that acts as the impetus of an entire community moving more deeply into union with God. This is what Francis of Assisi believed and lived.

In a time in which more formal and professional social service agencies are being established as parts of parishes and other church-related organizations, the need for a greater and more specific guiding principle that will effectively motivate competent service with meaningful ministry is critical. Without this kind of guiding principle the work of church-sponsored social outreach becomes very much like that of any non-sectarian agency providing similar services. In light of this observation, one is reminded of Francis' parting words encouraging his brothers to be fulfilled in the kind of work to which they were called; his message for ministers is not in what is being *done*, but how it is *shared*. For Franciscans to offer social service as a ministry is commendable, but the question remains: How does this ministry share the Franciscan charism?

Another consideration for church-sponsored social services is the development of staffs that reflect a certain mode of service. Increasingly, the staff of any such agency will be a collaborative effort between men and women, religious and the laity. The challenges and benefits of this are many. A critical piece in this reality is how the staff as a whole is moving toward a point of like-mindedness in the manner in which the agency serves. The embrace of a commonly held guiding principle is the catalyst for meaningful and significant service for the Church and the local community. While there is no particular theory for Franciscan ministry, the field of social work and social service offers what may be seen as a bridge between Franciscan spirituality and professional social outreach. One such model is the strengths perspective. In this theory there lie parallels to the goals of Francis and his ministry and the aforementioned meaningful and competent mode of social service.

The foundational principles of social work include the quality of identifying, eliciting, and substantiating the strengths of a client or population. Yet, historically, there has been a reliance on more psychoanalytical theories through the course of the profession's development that often takes a pathological or deficit-oriented approach. The role of the helping professional can often become that of one who brings limits to the treatment of a client through specific diagnoses and categorizations. Even with the presumed goodwill and professionalism of the social service provider there still often remains the oversight of the promise of client's possibility for accomplishment. Inasmuch, the strengths perspective serves as a theory focused on the client's growth, talents, and potential contribution to society. It aims to reflect Francis' own belief in the transformative power of cultivating an environment of meaningful relationships.

The strengths perspective is able to identify with two Franciscan ministerial qualities of being rooted in the personalisitic dimension as well as flowing out of the fraternal and communal character of Franciscan life[2]. As Dominic Monti, O.F.M., points out, the need for a common search and subsequent application of identified values further shapes and augments both the community and ministry. Similarly, when the strengths perspective is applied on the communal level (where it has significant effect) the individuals co-discerning their strengths respectively and collectively are positioned to fulfill the need for personalism, social responsibility and pluralism while forming community or a part of a community.

---

[2]See Dominic Monti, O.F.M., "Franciscan Ministry: Changing Contexts and Historical Develop-ments," *The Cord* 41/3 (March 1991).

The Impact of Pathology and Deficits

A new way of working with the poor of any social or personal condition (*vis a vis* traditional social services) can offer an enlivened sense of purpose for those served as well as those who serve. When assessments are based upon the pathological, the deficits often minimize the client's potential. The traditional medical model of focusing on the disease which has informed social services' emphasis on the dysfunction in the presenting problem seems only to "reinforce the powerlessness the client is already facing."[3] Working from this perspective can lead the service provider to underestimate the client's experience, the presence of untapped reserves of capacity, and the hope of change. In a sense the diagnostic outcome acts as a weight in the favor of the knowledge-based, pathology-oriented social service provider leaving the client in a possible continued state of helplessness. This kind of imbalance often only perpetuates dependence and powerlessness. The result is twofold. The first is the possible degradation of the client which only serves as a reinforcement of society's ill-treatment of the individual or specific population. The second is the loss of resources on a client or a single population bound to a label or diagnosis, rather than the process of providing healing and a mutually realized outcome by the social service and the client. This loss of resources also denies another client or segment of population in need from receiving services. In the management of resources the deficits model may beg the question whose needs are being served, the client or the agency? Inasmuch, the results deny a sense of mutuality and therefore any reflection of the idea of relationship as held by Francis.

The Strengths Perspective in Terms of Justice

In terms of justice, the strengths perspective serves the client more effectively in the relational dynamic with the social service provider. Approaching the healing relationship from the client's perspective allows a sense of empowerment to be established, and, therefore, a quality of justice. In doing so, the uniqueness of the clients' circumstances are validated, thus providing for a more personal and constructive place for the clients' goals to

---

[3]Charles D. Cowger, "Assessment of Client Strengths: Clinical Assessment for Client Empower-ment," *Social Work* 39/3 (May 1994): 262-68.

be realized. Cowger notes that "[c]linical practice based upon empowerment assumes the client power is achieved when clients make choices that give them control over their presenting problem and, in turn, their own lives."[4] The story of the wolf of Gubbio reflects this point by allowing the previously threatening animal to be "heard" so as to have its needs met by the townspeople while having their needs met. Inasmuch, justice is rendered through Francis' ministry.

The sense of justice derived from the strengths perspective also underscores its inherent commitment to personalism and pluralism. The value of the individual as well as the value of the differences and talents of many perspectives (social, cultural, lifestyle, physical, and mental capacities) are necessary in facilitating attentive ministry as well as realizing the potential outcomes of the strengths perspective. The richness Francis found in each person or community was part of the personalistic and pluralistic understanding he held for all creation. The critical criteria of justice issues in a ministerial plan or action are also reflected in the application of the strengths perspective.

Subsidiarity is inherently found in the strengths perspective. By addressing the needs and concerns of those joining the Franciscan ministry, the agency and the clients work on issues on a level that is non-hierarchical and avoid seeking direction or authority from any larger social construct. The subsequent form reinforces the social work value of self-determination. It also maintains a sense of comfort for those just entering a situation in which they are learning and later practicing power in the greater community. The negotiation between the wolf and the Gubbians serves as an example of subsidiarity where the two entities worked out the conditions for peace without the authority of a court. Francis served only as a facilitator and motivator in coming to a commonly subscribed agreement which both sides could uphold. The *Canticle* and the account of the leper similarly reflect dynamics of a shared realization of the importance of a balanced exchange of gifts. In each story the various participants collaborate equally and freely, thus finding their rightful and active place in the Kingdom.

---

[4] Cowger, 263.

The Elements of the Strengths Perspective

The path to personal or social wellness or recovery, therefore, needs to find power in the possibility to change rather than within the specter of reiterated dysfunction. The strengths perspective accesses a language of change centered on 1) empowerment and the suspension of disbelief; 2) membership, dialogue, collaboration and synergy; and 3) resilience, regeneration and healing from within.[5] Each of the three groupings of the strength perspective's qualities can be matched with the Franciscan ministerial values of peacemaking, community building, and mutual healing. The strengths perspective and Franciscan ministerial values considered together may be able to inform each other of a deeper realization of their respective and shared goals. In and of themselves they represent a relationship based on mutuality with a common goal of the uplifting of those who apply and benefit from them.

Empowerment and the Suspension of Disbelief: Franciscan Peace-making

Cowger indicates that empowerment "means not only that human beings possess the strengths and potential to resolve their own difficult life situations, but also that they increase their strength and contribute to society by doing so."[6] Others substantiate this point by elucidating that what occurs in the change process using the strengths perspective is not just an individual endeavor (as found in other therapeutic change processes).[7] It has political ramifications on group and community membership. They believe that by viewing it from a political standpoint the client or client population can refuse stereotypes or labels as well as eradicate their own oppression. By underscoring the individual's or group's power of change, there begins a healing process of movement away from traditional self-focused treatment toward community enhancement.

---

[5]See Dennis Saleebey, "Power to the People," *The Strengths Perspective in Social Work Practice*, ed. Dennis Saleebey (White Plains, NY: Longman, 1992), 3-17.

[6]Cowger, 19.

[7]David E. Pollio, Sharon M. McDonald, Carol S. North, "Combining a Strengths-Based Approach and Feminist Theory in Group Social Work with 'Persons on the Streets,'" *Social Work with Groups*, 19/3 & 4 (1996): 5-20.

Empowerment, as a key aspect of the strengths perspective, offers a holistic quality to this change process. Through the lens of social ecology the empowerment of the individual or group has a benefit for the larger community by the former's building competencies, taking control, assuming responsibilities and becoming involved.[8] Thus, what occurs on one level has an effect on the other. This point is based on the terms of mutuality and reciprocity: that personal or group change foments a community attitudinal adjustment. The eventuality is for the greater society to respond and reciprocally encourage the smaller, newly-empowered community.

In the strengths perspective the social service provider creates the space in which client empowerment can be fostered. The agency in its approach to a client or client group will research the needs of its members and the local community to form a more significant environment of change. The agency as a catalyst for change serves as a base from which clients and client groups can organize, focus and begin to move on their path toward empowerment. While encouraging the empowerment of the client base, the agency or social service provider will need to be mindful of transgressing the process with empowerment's antithesis of paternalism.[9] The professional coordination of the strengths perspective's operationalization is a guiding role, not a leading role. This stance offers facilitation, access to resources, and assistance in defining goals as well as providing motivation. De Jong and Miller add that "the client [or client group] is empowered by the [social] worker's creating a context that requires [them] to draw on two of [their] most important and unique human capacities: conceptualizing [their] own world and making decisions about how to live in it."[10]

As the facilitator of the strengths process, the social service provider initially may be perceived by those with whom this ministry is shared (i.e., the clientele) primarily as a reflection of social attitudes and biases. For empowerment to take root an environment of trust and confidence needs to be established. Francis in the role of the facilitator first shattered any resistance from the wolf when he extended himself as a trusting and trusted con-

---

[8]Julian Rappaport, Thomas M. Reischl, and Marc A. Zimmerman, "Mutual Help Mechanisms in the Empowerment of Former Mental Patients," *The Strengths Perspective in Social Work Practice*, ed. Dennis Saleebey (White Plains, NY: Longman, 1992), 84-97.

[9]Saleebey, "Beginnings of a Strengths Approach," makes this point by drawing on the observation of Carol Swift in her article "Empowerment: An Antidote to Folly" (1984).

[10]Peter De Jong and Scott D. Miller, "How to Interview for Client Strengths," *Social Work* 40/6 (1995): 734.

ciliator. As with the initial stages of a therapeutic alliance, Francis saw the wolf's vulnerability and powerlessness as an area of primary concern. The wolf was able to participate in Francis' healing process once it understood that Francis was working for the mutual advantage of both the wolf and the village. The wolf saw that its entry into the reconciliation process afforded it a sense of power. Similarly, addressing the larger community's feelings and actions (the Gubbian villagers) against the client (the wolf) as an ingrained and debilitating obstacle becomes part of the initial work of the strengths perspective. Therefore, a suspension of disbelief is the key to the facilitation or "opening up" of the clients and the preconceptions or biases of the larger community. This critical element in the empowerment of those served is in the listening and working with their perspectives by the agency or worker (the role of Francis), not as a fact-finding investigation or reminder of others' ill-perception of the clients. Rather, the necessity of belief in "their side of the story" by the agency (as Francis accorded the wolf) offers a validation of the clients' understanding of life while representing symbolically a community that can include clients' narrative in the greater social discourse. The process affords a first step for the clients who seek change while the greater community (represented in the agency) is listening, empathic and willing to respond. Francis' ministry of listening and providing a place to heal wounds and fractured relationships as with the wolf serve as models of this technique. Francis believed in the wolf's possibility of constructive engagement with the villagers, if not in the essential goodness of the wolf despite its history with the Gubbians. The social service provider's awareness of this point is taking "the shift [...] away from professional work as the exertion of power of knowledge...to professional work as collaborating with the power within the individual (or community) toward a life that is palpably better, and better in the clients' own terms.[11]

Rappaport, Reischl and Zimmerman adopted the 1989 definition from the Cornell University Empowerment Group: that empowerment is "an intentional, ongoing process centered in the local community, involving mutual respect, critical reflection, caring, and group participation, through which people lacking an equal share of valued resources gain greater access to and control over those resources."[12]

---

[11]Saleebey, "Beginnings of a Strengths Approach," 13.
[12]Rappaport et al., 85.

The spirit of mutuality and trust is found as a basis for the change process to take root when empowerment and a suspension of disbelief are put into action. Francis' careful and thoughtful negotiation with the wolf and the Gubbians was the concrete application of empowerment as a key to successful ministry.

Membership, Dialogue, Collaboration and Synergy: Franciscan Community Building

Four other principles in the strengths perspective are membership, dialogue, collaboration and synergy. Each principle plays a part not only in actualizing the potential in the client or client group, but also in their corporate unity-the area of greatest efficacy. These principles are rooted in empowerment and serve as facilitating processes in the greater strengths system. The *Canticle of Creation* represents the application of these principles in terms of a unity amongst all creation emanating from and reflecting the source of all being.

Membership is seen as an essential quality in constructing community and identity. Walzer sees that a "communal place and identity is an absolute requisite for the realization of distributive justice."[13] Similarly, Himes and Himes cite that there is no community where there is no justice.[14] The meaningful inclusion of all people in the social fabric erodes alienation and a sense of mutual suspicion while it builds justice in the social environment. The first encounter of membership can be found in the strengths perspective-based local social service agency through validation. By accepting the clients for who they are, the agency or service provider is that first experience of having the door opened to real membership in a form of community. For those who previously have not been extended membership in any context, acceptance and joining are powerful and transformative tools in the strengths process. The initial exchange of both sides being open to each other inculcates a spirit of solidarity between the social framework and the disenfranchised. By according membership and subsequently social partici-

---

[13]M. Walzer, *The Spheres of Justice* (New York: Basic Books, 1983) as quoted in Saleebey, "Beginnings to a Strengths Approach."
[14]Michael J. Himes and Kenneth R. Himes, *Fullness of Faith: The Public Significance of Theology* (NJ: Paulist Press, 1993).

pation, clients will begin constructing identities by contributing to the community into which they have become a part.

Membership, like empowerment, is a both a tool of justice and the strengths perspective. The impact of membership is therefore twofold: 1) the social service provider encourages a just community while 2) creating a social condition that the client or client population had not experienced until then. In recognizing each part of creation and appreciating the various elements of the universe, the *Canticle* offers an actualization of membership. Membership, as seen by Francis, is that necessary risk to be fully inclusive which is the single way to constructively establish peace through community building.

The next step in the process of the strengths perspective is the fostering of dialogue and collaboration between the new client/members and the larger community. Dialogue is a powerful dynamic in which the exchange of ideas, experiences, values and emotions are expressed in an atmosphere of trust and respect. The arrival of this point in the process is facilitated by the contributors' mutual acceptance of each other and their right to membership in the conversation. Francis as mystical poet joins all of creation in metaphor as he reflects the Creator's role in bringing the many created parts together simultaneously to act or work as a whole in an eternal conversation of love and fulfillment.

To be heard and to have the forum to speak are strong stances for those who previously were shut out from any significant expression in the public forum. Collaboration, as seen with the therapeutic alliance, may be seen as the action related to or based upon dialogue. The manner of working together to achieve a mutually conceived goal requires a collective imagination and will as the Creator provides in Francis' imagination. The increasingly empowered members in concert with the social service provider negotiate the terms of the project or situation on which they are collaborating. The power dynamic is further seen in terms of the horizontal as the parameters of a collaborative action are shared and mutually agreed upon. Collaboration may be seen as the fulfilling and equitable action (or expression of talents) of the *Canticle*'s call to unify for a greater sense of all creation.

Synergy is a result of membership, dialogue and collaboration when utilized fairly and with concern for the common good. The prospect of a synergistic force between the many members is the outcome of their willing and cooperative spirit to constructively engage a system or become a union of corresponding elements. The community, therefore, will utilize resources more efficiently and justly, while finding them expandable and renewable. With members working together, a mutually beneficial dynamic will be generated. The image of the Kingdom as perceived in the *Canticle* offers a synergistic reality on the greatest scale. Whether seen in terms of theology or social psychology, Francis' grasp of this necessary cooperation and unitive reality gives every social and spiritual hope of achieving the ultimate benefit of synergy which is peace.

Resilience, Regeneration and Healing from Within: Franciscan Mutual Healing

The concepts of resilience, regeneration and healing from within also serve as "perspectives of the possible" despite the seemingly overwhelming cir-cumstances faced by the disadvantaged and disenfranchised. The encounter of the leper serves as a metaphor for these strength perspective principles. Both the leper and Francis were seeking healing: one for physical needs, the other for the spiritual. Their respective endurance and their recognition of working together to achieve their respective goals of healing or transformation speak clearly to their resilience, regeneration, and the will to heal from within.

Resilience is that quality which has maintained a person's life force based upon hope. It is found in the intrinsic but not always discernible qualities of self-dignity and self-belief, as well as the will to survive. Regeneration is rooted in the bio-social-psycho makeup of a person to regain at least some level of what has been previously reduced or taken away. These two qualities are then seen as ingredients that foster the healing from within. An environment of self- and communal-healing is fortified by the support and care of others who can empathize and coordinate the process of fulfillment for a given individual. Because the strengths perspective is exercised in a community setting, a level of mutuality enables all the members to work for their respective and collective renewal. These qualities broke the isolation and alienation Francis and the leper suffered. Their collaboration was the impetus to begin a change process and to seize the opportunity to heal. These actions enabled each of them to begin a movement beyond their conditions; the prospect of growth was established beyond the possibility of what they may have realized on their own.

Resilience, regeneration and the healing from within are therefore inherent or innate but are most successfully brought to fruition by the larger group. Recent research is pointing toward this understanding in both medical and psychological circumstances. For the Franciscan minister this concept of healing is merely a confirmation of the healing presence of the community while also underscoring the value of the spiritual. What Francis demonstrated through his ministerial practices is a reflection of the strengths perspective: being rooted in the belief of unity of creation based in the appreciation and certain place of each part of creation working in fulfillment of itself and the universe.

Implications of Integrating Ministry and Social Services

The strengths perspective offers a unique understanding of how the suffering and pain of the needy may be ameliorated. Its essentially counter-cultural thrust reflects the possibility of healing and wholeness through the dynamic of meaningful relationship with the larger community. While it is not a specifically "Christian" or "Franciscan" theory, it appears to be compatible with the intentions of those local faith communities who strive to respond to their neighbors' needs while cultivating an atmosphere of right relationship. It intends to enrich those beyond the groups served, in that it models for the larger (secular) community how effective and caring services can be provided.

The counter-cultural aspect of the strengths perspective can facilitate the healing, peacemaking and community building of Franciscan ministry. In realizing the environment in which the strengths perspective strives to take root, the dynamic of ministry may be further enriched. As a tool toward this goal, the perspective offers the possibility of all concerned in an ministerial endeavor to attempt to fulfill the call to serve, participate in fortifying relationships and build a spirit of unity so desired by our Creator. Obviously it is not the sole way to engage a community seeking to live out the Gospel. It does propose that by building constructive and mutual relationships in a supportive and encouraging environment with specific principles and a certain focus, a form of community can be enhanced which can bear a resemblance to the Kingdom as imagined by St. Francis.

William Margraf is a former member of the Holy Name Province of the Order of Friars Minor. He holds an M.S.W. degree from the School of Social Work at the Catholic University of America in Washington, D.C. Currently he is employed as a social worker on the upper west side of Manhatten in New York City.

Reflection Questions

1. In your particular ministry, what is the possible application of the "strengths perspective" as a means to fulfill the dual mission of the agency's work and a Franciscan place of ministry?

2. How does your Franciscan place of ministry work with the conventions of knowledge-oriented and pathology-oriented professions in light of the ministry's Franciscan charism?

3. In the arena of meaningful practice, what is critical to your ministry in terms of offering both professional services while fulfilling the description of the ministry as Franciscan?

4. The challenge of both the strengths perspective and Franciscan ministerial values is rooted in their counter-cultural approach to their respective and cooperative work. How does the prophetic element of ministry factor into the daily work life of your place of ministry? What are the immediate and local risks that an integration of the strengths perspective and Franciscan ministry bring to your ministry or agency? What are the benefits and limitations such an integration would place upon your ministry or agency?

References

Blastic, M.W. "A Franciscan Approach to Ministry." *The Cord* 41/3 (1991): 80-88.

Cowger, C.D. "Assessing Client Strengths: Clinical Assessment for ClientEmpowerment." *Social Work* 39/3 (1994): 262-68.

De Jong, P. & S.D. Miller. "How to Interview for Client Strengths." *Social Work:* 40/6 (1995): 729-736.

Hepworth, D.H. & J.A Larsen. *Direct Social Work Practice (Fourth dition).*Pacific Grove, CA: Brooks/Cole Publishing Co., 1993.

Himes, M. & K. Himes. *Fullness of Faith: The Public Significance of Theology.* New York/Mahwah, N.J.: Paulist Press, 1993.

Joseph, M. V. & Conrad, A.P. "A Parish Neighborhood Model for Social Work Practice." *Social Casework: The Journal of Contemporary Social Work* (Sept. 1980): 423-32.

Leclerc, E. *Song of Dawn.* Chicago: Franciscan Herald Press, 1977.

Monti, Dominic. "Franciscan Ministry-Changing Contexts and HistoricalDevelopments." *The Cord* 41/3 (1991): 66-79.

Morrison, J.D., Howard, J., Johnson, C., Navarro, F.J., Plachetka, B., and Bell, T. "Strengthening Neighborhoods by Developing Community Networks." *Social Work* 42/5 (1997): 527-34.

Rappaport, J., Reischl, T.M., & Zimmerman, M. "Mutual Help Mechanisms in the Empowerment of Former Mental Patients." In D. Saleebey (Ed.), *The Strengths Perspective In Social Work Practice.* White Plains, N.Y.: Longman, 1992.

Reamer, F.G. *The Philosophical Foundations Of Social Work.* New York: Columbia University Press, 1993.

Saleebey, D. "The Strengths Perspective In Social Work Practice: Extensions And Cautions." *Social Work* 41/3 (1996): 296-305.

Saleebey, D. "Culture, Theory, And Narrative: The Intersection of Meanings In Practice." *Social Work* 39/4 (1994): 351-59.

Saleebey, D. "Introduction: Beginnings Of A Strengths Approach To Practice." In D. Saleebey (Ed.), *The Strengths Perspective In Social Work Practice.* White Plains, N.Y.: Longman, 1992.

Walzer, M. (1983). *Spheres of Justice.* New York: Basic Books. In Saleebey, D. (Ed.), *The Strengths Perspective Of Social Work Practice* White Plains, N.Y.: Longman, 1991.

Weick, A. Rapp, C. Sullivan, W.P., & Kisthardt, W. (1989). "A Strengths Perspective For Social Work Practice." *Social Work* 7/89 (1989): 350-54.

Penitential Humanism:
Rereading The Sources to Develop a Franciscan Urban Spirituality

Joseph P. Chinnici, O.F.M.

Introduction

Welcome the *city*. By choosing to live there, you welcome its rhythms, laws, problems, tragedies, difficulties, and holiness. Bound up like this with its life, your life-style and faith should make you credible in its eyes. As silver is smelted in a crucible, so will you be smelted in the heart of the city, like Christ in Jerusalem.[1]

These words emerged from the heart of a post-Vatican II Christian striving to give witness to the Gospel in the center of a post-industrial city. Father Pierre-Marie Delfieux, after an initial experience as chaplain at the Sorbonne, spent two years as a hermit in the Sahara desert and began slowly to realize that a new space of conversion opened out before the contemporary person: the space of the cities, "Paris, London, New York, Kinshasa, Tokyo, São Paolo, Cairo, and Mexico."[2] It was there, he believed, in the midst of the poor, in places of isolation and anonymity, spiritual thirst and physical hunger, that the quest for holiness in the modern world finds its true challenge. Under his leadership, the Monastic Fraternities of Jerusalem (one for men, one for women) formed in the center of Paris in 1975-1976. The rule of life indicates that the members express their solidarity with the world of the urban poor by entering the workforce five days a week, living in tenant buildings, and attracting a broad range of members with different forms of affiliation: brothers and sisters living in community, single people living alone, family group members, and lay adherents.[3]

---

[1] *The Jerusalem Community Rule of Life*, foreword by Carlo Carretto (Mahwah, New Jersey: Paulist Press, 1985), #41.

[2] Pierre-Marie Delfieux, "The Desert Today," *The Way* 27 (July 1987): 184-91, with quotation from 188.

[3] *The Jerusalem Community Rule of Life*, "Introduction" by Dom James Leachman, O.S.B., x.

Influenced strongly by the Benedictine tradition, the *Rule of Life* incorporates elements from the early desert monasticism of St. Basil, the modern quest of Charles de Foucauld, and the Carmelite Sister Elizabeth of the Trinity. Witness to the universality of the Christian message (love of God, love of neighbor), the dignity of every person as an image of God, work as a creative activity for the building up of the human family are here coupled with the practices of monastic asceticism which would foster this life: prayer, silence, humility, and the traditional triad of poverty, chastity, and obedience. The purpose is witness in the heart of the city:

> Learn, too, to contemplate the beauty and holiness of the city where God resides and where he has placed you. There, at the heart of the city, raise your arms in praise and intercession, call down his blessing on it each day and praise the Most High for all holy men and women who live in it and sanctify it.[4]

This very contemporary attempt to develop a positive spiritual witness in the midst of the modern city is not isolated. New urban hermits and communities of reconciliation and spiritual discipline are emerging in England, Canada, the United States and elsewhere.[5] While receiving inspiration from ancient monasticism, as does the Jerusalem Community, these efforts are also directly occasioned by acute experiences of urban poverty and violence. Most recently, a survey of the revitalization attempts within Protestant and Roman Catholic parochial structures has been conducted in eleven different cities in order to understand common patterns associated with successful urban spiritual renewal. "There is a positive turning away from a sense of dependence and disengagement," this study concludes:

> toward affirmation of religious inner strength, identification of indigenous assets, local leadership, social cohesion through faith-based community, a new sense of empowerment, trust in

---

[4]*The Jerusalem Community Rule of Life*, #130.
[5]See for examples Eileen Mary, "Desert or Mountain-Top or City," *The Way, Supplement* 59 (Summer 1987): 14-23; Theresa Mancuso, "The Urban Hermit: Monastic Life in the City," *Review for Religious* 55 (March/April 1996): 133-42; for broader trends see Charles A. Fracchia, *Living Together Alone: The New American Monasticism* (San Francisco: Harper & Row, 1979), and *Second Spring, the Coming of Age of U.S. Catholicism* (San Francisco: Harper & Row, 1980).

the staying power of the church for the long-term, increased capacity for new partnerships, a deeper sense of human dignity and self-worth, a renewed practice of caring for one's neighbor, and confidence for shaping the future in a way that is more just and life-affirming.[6]

The synthesis of these numerous case studies has coincided with historical essays which detail the contribution religious belief has made to helping people negotiate the changing urban landscape, to "conquer" it, so to speak, through community formation around common stories, symbols, alliances, and projects.[7]

In the last few years members of the Franciscan family and others skilled in urban ministry and its challenges have gathered in Denver to discuss how Franciscans themselves might contribute to this widespread rethinking of the Church's urban ministry and presence. Much has been learned about how to approach this contemporary situation and we continue a dialogue that has been building within the Franciscan community for several years.[8] By interacting with representatives of various disciplines, those knowledgeable and skilled in urban work and criminal justice, those fully aware of the institutional barriers within the Church to social equality and advocacy, and scholar practitioners in preaching and social justice, I have seen the importance of trying to approach our Franciscan sources in a new way. Certainly, we are used to emphasizing the values of minority and fraternity, but these need to be interpreted in such a way in our preaching and action so as to speak to the contemporary urban scene. Our Franciscan language of community, the vows, and mission must be developed in such a way as to break out of its religious ghetto and engage the secular world from within. The vows and ascetical practices of our tradition must be reinterpreted as "therapies of the self-in-community," disciplines which enable us to live within the stresses and strains of urban violence and conflict without succumbing to its addictions and passions. Bridges need to be built. The city of God and the

---

[6]See Nile Harper, *Urban Churches, Vital Signs, Beyond Charity Toward Justice* (Grand Rapids, Michigan: William B. Eerdmans, 1999), with long quotation from page 10.

[7]Most recently, Robert A. Orsi, ed., *Gods of the City, Religion and the American Urban Landscape* (Bloomington and Indianapolis: Indiana University Press, 1999).

[8]See for examples, Anthony M. Carrozzo, O.F.M., *Refounding in the Franciscan Tradition, Spirit and Life, A Journal of Contemporary Franciscanism* 5 (1994); Ramona Miller, OSF, "Theological Reflections for Ministry as Franciscan," *The Cord* 47 (March-April 1997): 57-63.

communal city of the person need to be joined in a new synthesis of theological, social, and political humanism.

It has become clear to me that connections can easily be made between
theories of social work as empowerment, the liberation of client strengths
and the content of Franciscan preaching. In addition, as Patricia Keefe ar-
gues in this volume, our own value of poverty can be seen as one that cri-
tiques dominant economic structures and institutional prejudices so as to
stand for justice and the freedom and dignity of the person. Our sources,
when read in a certain way, do address the values of human work, active engagement in political processes, and the universalist dimensions of the Gospel. It is possible to break out of a narrowly religious reading of Francis'
writings and see them, so to speak, from the outside, for their broader social
meaning.[9]

Contemporary European studies, usually by laymen and women, are
attempting just that type of reading.[10] In what follows, I explore how our
Franciscan sources, especially the writings of Francis himself, can be framed
in such as way as to engage this new secular world. First, I would identify the
importance of this task within the context of contemporary American Catholicism. In part two, I describe the urban crusade of Francis' own time.
The paper concludes with a broad description of a new "ideology of Franciscan life,"[11] a penitential humanism in which we speak about ourselves and

---

[9] The narrowness of the traditional interpretation of Franciscan themes emerges very
clearly from recent historical studies of the thirteenth century. See in particular *Dalla "Sequela
Christi" di Francesco d'Assisi all "Apologia della Povertà,"* Atti del XVIII Covegno Internazionale
(Assisi, 18-20 Ottobre 1990), Spoleto, 1992. For some notable reinterpretations see Ovidio
Capitani, "Verso una nuova antropologia e una nuova religiosita," in *La Conversione alla Povertà
nell'Italia dei Secoli XII-XIV,* Atti del XVII Convegno storico internazionale (Todi, 14-17 Otto-
bre, 1990), Spoleto, 1991, 447-71; Thadée Matura, OFM, "Una Sola Vocación, Una Solo
Carisma, Una Sola Familia," *Selecciones de Franciscanismo* (1993): 201-10.

[10] The presentation has been significantly influenced by the following studies: Giovanna
Casagrande, *Religiosita Penitentziale e Citta al Temo dei Communi* (Rome: Capuchin Historical
Institute, 1995), who refers to the phrase "penitential humanism" of P. Marangon, 117; Ovidio
Capitani, "Verso una nuova antropologia e una nuova religiosità"; Enrico Menesto, "Per Una
Riletura della *Epistola ad Fideles* di San Francesco d'Assisi," in *Santi e Santita nel Movimento
Penitenziale Francesco dal Duecento al Cinquecento,* ed. Lino Temperini (Rome: Editrice Analecta
TOR, 1998), 9-23; Jacques LeGoff, "Franciscanisme et Modèles Culturels du XIII Siecle," in
Francescanesimo e Vita Religiosa dei Laici Nel '200, Atti dell'VIII Convegno Internazionale [16-18
Ottobre 1980] (Assisi: Società internazionale di studi francescani, 1981), 85-128; David Flood,
OFM, *Work for Everyone, Francis of Assisi and the Ethic of Service* (Quezon City, Philippines:
CCFMC Office, 1997).

[11] For the use of the term "ideology" and its signficance see Patricia Wittberg S.C., *The
Rise and Fall of Catholic Religious Orders, A Social Movement Perspective* (NY: The State University
of New York Press, 1994), 13-42.

our mission from within the experience of a multi-cultural, heterogeneous, ecumenical, and secular environment which is the modern city.

The Changing Context of American Catholicism

Our practical experiments and historical reflections on urban spirituality come at a much-needed time within the American Catholic community. The changing demographics of the community itself, the new face of poverty, the developments in communal liturgical life, and the attempts to move beyond the ethnic-neighborhood base of the immigrant Church by embarking on vast programs of inner-city parochial consolidation and restructuring have led to a great deal of both soul-searching and creative wondering about a new vision for Catholic urban ministry.[12] For example, David Fukyzawa's study of these developments in the city of Detroit reveals a pattern not untypical of the Church as a whole. He describes the challenges to the Church posed by inner-city racial and ethnic communities, the closing of schools, the loss of urban jobs and the emergence of the chronically poor, the population's shift to the suburbs, and the decline in the number of priests. A task force formed in the early 1980s by the Detroit archdiocese noted that the urban environment called for the development of "small, viable, multicultural communities of faith"; it provided opportunity for the emergence of lay ministries, culturally specific works, and the encouragement of new partnerships in the Church's assumption of greater "civic responsibility."[13] In a similar fashion, Archbishop Rembert Weakland, in an address at a conference sponsored by the National Pastoral Life Center in

---

[12]For an overview see especially Jay P. Dolan, "American Catholics in a Changing Society: Parish and Ministry, 1930 to the Present," in Dolan, R. Scott Appleby, Patricia Byrne, and Debra Campbell, *Transforming Parish Ministry, The Changing Roles of Catholic Clergy, Laity, and Women Religious* (New York: Crossroad, 1989), 283-320; Frederick J. Perella Jr., "Roman Catholic Approaches to Urban Ministry, 1945-85," in Clifford J. Green, ed., *Churches, Cities, and Human Community, Urban Ministry in the United States, 1945-85* (Grand Rapids, Michigan: William B. Eerdmans, 1996). For specific examples: Diocese of Oakland, "The Challenge of Urban Ministry," *Origins* 15 (August 15, 1985): 156-60; David E. DeCosse, "The Case of Our Lady of Sorrows, Success & Catholic Inner-City Schools," *Commonweal* CXIV (April 10, 1987): 210-15; James R. Lund & Mary L. Heidkamp, "Parish Models for Social Action," *Church* 7 (Summer 1991): 29-32; Patricia Natali Lamoureux, "Parish Twinning: Beyond Chairty," *Church* 8 (Fall 1992): 36-39; Joseph Claude Harris, "The Shrinking Church in Big Cities," *Church* 10 (Fall 1994): 28-30.

[13]David Fukuzawa, "Developing a Strategy for the Urban Parish: The Lessons of the Church Closings in Detroit," *New Theology Review* (February 6 1993): 54-65, with quotes from pages 58, 63.

1996, outlined the following multi-dimensional program for the Church's response to the new urban poor:

- In a situation where there is little hope of betterment in the plight of the poor, the Church needs, first of all, to reiterate the fidelity of God's love and providence by preaching "the inherent worth of the poor and thus that they should have hope ...".
- In a situation where the problems of poverty are so intricately related to the availability of work, the Church needs to collaborate with others, both ecumenically and politically, in advocacy for job creation, decent wages, healthy labor conditions, and education.
- In a situation of increasing violence, the Church needs to develop programs to safeguard the family by preaching against domestic violence, arguing for fairness in society, and developing programs to prevent pregnancies outside of marriage.[14]

It is clear from all of these examples that as the Church in the United States moves into the third millennium, it is faced with an urban pastoral situation not unlike that which is emerging internationally. Creative forms of communal sharing, more broadly-based alliances, universalist dimensions of theology, spirituality, and practice, and new tools for evangelization are demanded. The city clearly has provided both challenge and opportunity as the cultural matrix from which the Christian life is embodied. Can we Franciscans rethink our own sources and spiritual tradition from within the context of these challenges?

Francis of Assisi and the Campaign for the City

Recent interpretations of the era which gave birth to Francis of Assisi have revealed the difficult problems posed by the urban society of his time. Lauro Martines has analyzed what she calls the "forms of violence" present in the thirteenth century Italian city, violence rooted in popular insurrections, civil war, pitched street battles, and political rivalries. The very layout of the city, with its narrow streets, large homes, open market, fortified cas-

---

[14]Archbishop Rembert Weakland, "The Urban Poor and the Churches," *Origins* 26 (November 14, 1996): 360-64.

tles, and dense neighborhoods invited violence. The influx of new people, wandering exiles, and the presence of the poor created an atmosphere of unrest. With no single authority capable of asserting its control, political rivalry was the order of the day. In such an atmosphere people struggled to protect their social privileges, to reclaim rights which had been denied, to establish mechanisms of control over their opponents. Martines compiles a list of "modes of political violence": frank and sustained refusal to heed the laws of the commune; formation of secret associations; incitements to riots; armed attacks on political figures; destruction of property; and physical assaults on ecclesiastical dignitaries. Suspicion, duplicity, doubt, anger, and conspiracy fractured human relationships. "Too often, in the thirteenth century Italian city," she writes, "doing the restrained or 'peaceful thing' would have required the renunciation of self-identity."[15]

In a parallel study, Alexander Murray describes the interplay of piety and impiety in the contexts of Milan, Padua, Pistoia, Pisa, Florence, and Verona. Using extant sermons, he identifies the trio of lust, pride, and avarice as the dominant vices assailing the new societies and notes the following evidences of "lack of faith": antipathy to sacred holidays because of business practices and the lure of commercial attractions; the neglect of sacramental confession; the dominance of habitual activities leading to the neglect of questions of eternal salvation; doubts regarding the eucharist and resurrection; denial of the afterlife; and the difficulty of believing in providence.[16] Studies of the suffering caused by bodily existence itself (sickness, poverty, hunger, starvation, the pains of child bearing and birthing, and omnipresent death) as the urban seedbed for the Cathar movement confirm that such difficulties pervaded the world of Francis of Assisi.[17] Economic exploitation, social division, violence, unbelief, and hatred of the human condition itself: such was the atmosphere which gave impetus to the Gospel poverty move-

---

[15]Lauro Martines, "Political Violence in the Thirteenth Century," in Martines, ed., *Violence and Civil Disorder in Italian Cities 1200-1500* (Berkeley: University of California Press, 1972), 331-53, with quotation from page 352. For an application to Assisi see Arnaldo Fortini, *Francis of Assisi*, translated by Helen Moak (New York: Crossroad, 1981), *passim*.

[16]Alexander Murray, "Piety and Impiety in Thirteenth-Century Italy," in G.J. Cuming and Derek Baker, *Popular Belief and Practice* (Cambridge: Cambridge University Press, 1972), 83-106.

[17]Raoul Manselli, *Francesco E I Suoi Compagni*, especially "San Francesco dal dolore degli uomini al Cristo crocifisso," 183-200, and "San Francesco e l'eresia," 235-55; Manselli, *Studi Sulle Eresie del Secolo XII*, (Rome: Capuchin Historical Institute, 1995), especially "Dolore e Morte Nell'Esperienza Religiosa Catara," 221-236; Carol Lansing, *Power & Purity, Cathar Heresy in Medieval Italy* (New York: Oxford 1998).

ments and actual birth to the formation of a "community of penitents" from Assisi. Such also were the concerns of the Church of the time.

When Innocent III ascended the papal throne in 1198 the urban unrest of central Italy and the struggle with Frederick II over control of the region was a crucial concern. The military battle with the emperor and the communes is well known, but as part of his strategy the new pope also quickly set about trying to pacify the region and develop a plan of social and moral reform.[18] In sermon after sermon Innocent narrated the spiritual and temporal ills of the people: heresy, carnal concupiscence, worldly inducements, and civil discord. The city needed to be surrounded by the four walls of prudence, justice, fortitude and temperance, and the gifts of the Holy Spirit needed to become the towers of the soul. Care for material concerns needed to be accompanied by equal care for spiritual things.[19] To accomplish this reform the pope appointed apostolic men called *rectores*, agents of his policy, to keep watch, to become the true custodians of city life.[20] He sent circular letters to Spoleto, Foligno, Assisi, Rieti, Narni, and elsewhere. Regretting his inability to be everywhere because of "the weakness of the human condition," Innocent called on the local bishops, who had sworn to him "obedience and reverence," to cooperate in his plan.[21] Underlying his appeals was a universalist ecclesiology, the conception of the Church as one people under a visible head with a global extension.[22]

Francis of Assisi grew up in this atmosphere which called for spiritual and temporal reform in the city-states of central Italy. From the time of his trip to Rome in 1209, when he probably took his oath of "reverence and obedience" to Innocent III, he specifically aligned himself with the many evangelical aspirations of the pope.[23] One of Francis' little studied and

---

[18]For Innocent's policies see Brenda Bolton, "'Except the Lord Keep the City,': towns and the papal states at the turn of the twelfth century," in David Abulafia, Michael Franklin, Miri Rubin, eds., *Church and City 1000-1500, Essays in Honor of Christopher Brooke* (Cambridge: Cambridge University Press, 1992) 199-218. This paragraph is greatly indebted to her research.

[19]PL, 217: 601-606.

[20]PL, 217: 603: *"Custodes civitatis sunt rectores Ecclesiae, sancti apostolici et apostolici viri, de quibus sponsa dicit in Canticis: "Invenerunt me vigiles qui custodiunt civitatem.""*

[21]PL 214: 751-752. For application to Assisi see also Fortini, *Francis of Assisi*, 226.

[22]See Michele Maccarrone, *Nuovi Studi Su Innocenzo III*, ed. Roberto Lambertini (Rome: Antonianum, 1995), 272-73.

[23]See for background and interpretation Michele Maccarrone, "S. Francesco e La Chiesa di Innocenzo III," in *Approccio Storico-Critico alle Fonti Francescane*, eds. G.C. e M.C. (Rome: Antonianum, 1979) 31-43; Pietro Zerbi, "San Francesco d'Assisi e la Chiesa Romena," in *"Ecclesia in hoc mundo posita" Studi di storia e di storiografia medioevale raccolti in occasione del 70 genetliaco dell'autore*, ed. Maria Pia Alberzoni (Milan: Vita e Pensiero), 355-84.

shorter writings is his *Epistola ad Populorum Rectores*, or *Letter to the Rulers of the People*, composed sometime around 1220.[24] In it Francis chooses words reflective of both the papal crusade for urban reform and the urban government structures and social needs of the time. Addressed to all "mayors and consuls, magistrates and governors" (*universis potestatibus et consulibus, iudicibus atque rectoribus*), "and to all others," those people who presided over the citizens in matters of war and peace, property and business, local and territorial concerns, the text is meant to have a universal appeal. In a parallel letter to the custodians of the friars written at the same time, Francis asks that they circulate this "*Letter to the Rulers*" to a very wide audience. Francis reminds the civil rulers of the approaching day of death; in a decidedly apocalyptic tone, he calls them to repentance. They live, as the twentieth century theologian Johannes Metz would say, within "bounded time," a time which will end in judgment, a time, therefore, which calls for change, for personal and social reform.[25]

In the ecclesiastical language of the thirteenth century Church, a language redolent of an appeal for social reconstruction and responsibility for the poor, Francis challenges his listeners to lay aside worldly cares and anxieties, those interior dispositions associated with the new market economy, the lure of riches, avarice, cupidity, the manipulation of others for the sake of one's own gain, the passions driving the citizenry towards violence.[26] The sign of this reform is the reception of the "Body and Blood of our Lord Jesus Christ," which ritually means alliance with the Church, the rejection of the garment of the world and the conversion to the way chosen by our Lord Jesus Christ when he became a human being, the way of engagement with the world of the poor. He concludes the letter in this fashion: "May you foster such honor to the Lord among the people entrusted to you that every evening an announcement may be made by a messenger or some other sign

---

[24]The Latin text can be found in *Fontes Franciscani*, eds. di Enrico Menesto and Stefano Brufani (Assisi: Edizioni Porziuncula, 1995), 107-108, with the English translation in Regis J. Armstrong, O.F.M.Cap., J.A. Wayne Hellmann, O.F.M. Conv., William J. Short, O.F.M., *Francis of Assisi: Early Documents: The Saint*, Vol. I (New York: New City Press, 1999), 58-59. For the text of "The Second Letter to the Custodians" see *Fontes*, 69.

[25]See Johann Baptist Metz, *A Passion for God, The Mystical-Political Dimension of Christianity*, translated by J. Matthew Ashley (Mahwah, New Jersey: Paulist Press, 1998), 72-91.

[26]For further elaboration of this interpretation see Joseph P. Chinnici, O.F.M., "Conflict and Power: The Retrieval of Franciscan Spirituality for the Contemporary Pastoral Leader," in Anthony Carrozzo. O.F.M., Vincent Cushing, O.F.M., Kenneth Himes, O.F.M., eds., *Franciscan Leadership in Ministry, Spirit and Life, A Journal of Contemporary Franciscanism* 7 (1997): 205-25; David Flood, ed., *Poverty in the Middle Ages* (Werl/Westf: Dietrich-Coelde-Verlag, 1975).

that praise and thanksgiving may be given by all people to the all-powerful Lord God."[27]

The appeal Francis makes in this letter to the mayors and magistrates has definite parallels in several other writings, most notably his *Exhortations to All the Faithful* (I and II), the sample sermon which the friars may give to the people (*Earlier Rule*, XXI), and the life of penance to which the brothers with all the "orders" in the Church need to adhere (*Earlier Rule*, XXIII.7). The same signs of conversion, love of God and love of neighbor, the same call to praise God, the same rituals of fidelity to the "footprints of Our Lord Jesus Christ" in the eucharist, the same commitment to the engagement with the historical inequities of their time, and the same consciousness of living under judgment is to be embraced by all. It is a common life oriented towards human, social, political, and religious reconstruction within the context of unbelief, violence, economic exploitation, social division, and hatred of the human condition. In the context of the city, this is the meaning of "doing penance," and the message is framed in such a way as to give specifically religious symbolism (the sacraments of eucharist and penance) a universalist interpretation. In contemporary terms, adherence to this ecclesial program of life produces human liberation, community, peace, and justice. As some historians would argue, Francis is here presenting a profile of the "new religious person"; he is arguing for a "new anthropology"; he is witnessing to a "new way of being human" in the world of his time.[28] We could identify this overall approach as one of a "penitential humanism" composed of a vision, a code of behavior, and strategies for enactment.

---

[27]Here Francis' interpretation of the eucharistic action of Christ, the assumption of the condition of being human, that is, poor and humble, is central. Confer *A Letter to the Entire Order*, 26-29. For further elaboration, see David Flood, O.F.M., *Francis of Assisi and the Franciscan Movement* (Quezon City, Philippines: The Franciscan Institute of Asia, 1989), 147 and *passim*.

[28]See, as previously mentioned, Ovidio Capitani, "Verso una nuova antropologia," and Giovanna Casagrande, *Religiosita Penitentziale*. Also moving in the same direction, although from different disciplines, are Ida Magli, *Gli Uomini della Penitenza* (Padua: Franco Muzzio, 1995); Thadée Matura, O.F.M., *The Message in His Writings*, translated by Paul Barrett, O.F.M. Cap. (Franciscan Institute Publications, 1997); Chiara Frugoni, *Francis of Assisi* (London: SCM Press, 1998).

Towards A Penitential Humanism

In an essay of this size, it is impossible to detail all of the component parts of Francis' "penitential humanism" as a response to the urban social conditions of his time. Certainly, the orientation itself calls for a reconsideration of the basic theological and canonical structures of interpretation which have supported our institutionalizations of fraternity (First, Second, and Third Orders; separate male and female, religious and lay worlds); the vows (poverty, chastity, obedience as the marks of religious consecration and distinction); the sacraments (the confinement of "real presence" and "forgiveness" to ecclesiastical rites); the Church (Roman allegiance as **the** distinguishing characteristic of Francis' spirituality); asceticism (interpreted in clerical and enclosed monastic terms); and mission (defined largely in terms of apostolic works related to local diocesan structures).[29] Dominic Monti's essay in this volume indicates how the Observant reform attempted in a similar fashion to break from the dominant communal forms of its time.[30] In what follows, let me simply try to delineate some general orientations underlying a "penitential humanism." They could be called "starting points for reflection."

The Vision

Penitential humanism begins with a universalist focus, consciously trying to formulate the religious project in terms which unite rather than divide people. Responding to the problems of social discord and violence, the focus shifts towards that which is common, human, shared by all persons by the mere fact of their existence. Framed in a society which questions the very value of certain human beings and experiences materiality itself as problematic, Francis' own conversion towards the human, which fundamentally began when the Lord led him to draw the leper into the orbit of the commu-

---

[29]This more thorough reconsideration is based on the fact that, as the cultural anthropologist Mary Douglas would argue, a change in classification means a change in worldview, purpose, and institution. Recent studies of the course of Franciscan history indicate that this "reclassification" has been a consistent struggle from the thirteenth century to the present. Cf. Douglas, *How Institutions Think* (NY: Syracuse University Press, 1986); Roberto Lambertini, Andrea Tabarroni, *Dopo Francesco: L'Eredità Difficile* (Turin: Gruppo Abele, 1989); Maria Pia Alberzoni et al., *Francesco d'Assisi e il primo secolo di storia francescana* (Turin: Einaudi, 1997).

[30]See Monti, "Franciscan Life and Urban Life: A Tense Relationship" in this volume.

nity,[31] received great institutional support from his allegiance to the universal pastoral project, the global *"curam et solicitudinem"* of Innocent III. This combination of identification with suffering humanity and the ecclesiological aspirations of the Holy See served as a potent mix, opening up his thought and action beyond the inherited structures of religious and pastoral life.[32]

This global vision of humanity surfaces many times in Francis' writings and actions. Most people are familiar with the importance of the visit to the Sultan, the non-Christian, and the witness which should be given when "going among the Saracens."[33] But these actions are rooted in themes present from the beginning of the conversion; particularly evident in both versions of the *Exhortation to the Brothers and Sisters of Penance.*[34] In the context of the canonical divisions of the Gregorian Church and the "forms of social violence," Francis' message is designed to vindicate the dignity of the person, to open up to all people (men and women, religious and lay) the possibility of following a Gospel way of life, to make available to everyone the option of living a Trinitarian mystical life. People, even those riddled with unbelief, become here not the objects of pastoral care but the very agents of social and religious change; there is no separation between being a human being and the possibility of being "spouse, mother, and brother" of the Lord Jesus Christ. Francis does not have one program for women and another for men: for both he has a single *propositum.* The writings communicate this vision by the simple use of words: The *Earlier Exhortation* is addressed to "all"; the *Later Admonition* and *Exhortation* "to all Christian and religious people: clergy and laity, men and women, and to all who live in the whole world"; the *Earlier Rule* appeals to "all people, races, tribes, and tongues, all nations and all peoples everywhere on earth, who are and who will be ...,"

---

[31]For a significant anthropological interpretation of the general context see Mark Gregory Pegg, "Le Corps et L'Autorité: la Lèpre de Baudouin IV," *Annales ESC* (Mars-Avril 1990) 2: 265-87.

[32]More and more historians are placing Francis' project in counter-distinction to the pastorally limited structures associated with the Gregorian Church. See, most prominently, Giovanni Miccoli, *Francesco d'Assisi, Realtà e memoria di un'esperienza cristiana* (Turin: Einaudi, 1991).

[33]For a recent interpretation see J. Hoeberichts, *Francis and Islam* (Quincy, Illinois: Franciscan Press, 1997).

[34]For commentary on these important texts see Leonard Lehmann, O.F.M. Cap., "Exultation and Exhortation to Penance: A Study of the Form and Content of the First Version of the *Letter to the Faithful,*" *Greyfriars Review* 4/2 (1990): 1-33; Flood, *Work for Everyone*; Menesto, "Per Una Rilletrura...."

"every creature"; "all peoples"; "all things temporal and spiritual."[35] As Jacques Dalarun would argue, "The term 'humanity' has no part in the lexicon of the thirteenth century. We rightly search for this word. 'All Christians' are the object of the *Letter to the Faithful*."[36]

It is noteworthy that both *Exhortations* contain in them a linguistic shift which indicates that Francis himself, one who has already embarked on a specifically religious way of life, identifies with his listeners on the primary level of their humanity. Beginning with the terms "all those who love the Lord" and the blessings that will come upon "all" when they do penance, Francis then changes terms to "we." The same shift occurs in the long chapter of prayer and thanksgiving in the *Earlier Rule* (Chapter 23). This underlying principle of identification also illuminates Francis' concentration throughout his writings on those key life passages which people share in common: birth, "going along the way," death. In the context of a Catharism which denies the goodness of material existence, Francis affirms as "good" those experiences which are fundamental to humanity itself. His writings juxtapose in a curious but clarifying way both the grandeur and horror of being human. The most famous example is *Admonition V*:

> Consider, O human being, in what great excellence the Lord God has placed you, for He created and formed you *to the image* of His beloved Son according to the body and *to His likeness* according to the Spirit.
>
> And all creatures under heaven serve, know, and obey their Creator, each according to its own nature, better than you. And even the demons did not crucify Him, but you, together with them, have crucified Him and are still crucifying Him by delighting in vices and sins.[37]

Using language which identifies beginning with conditions and experiences which are fundamentally human and then finding a common base of

---

[35] See *Earlier Exhortation* and *Later Admonition and Exhortation* (*Letters to the Faithful I & II*) and *Earlier Rule* 21.1, 23.1, 7.

[36] Dalarun, *Francesco: un passaggio, Donna e donne negli scritti e nelle leggende di Francesco d'Assisi* (Rome: Viella, 1994), 145.

[37] See commentary in Norbert Nguyen-Van-Khanh, O.F.M., *The Teacher of His Heart, Jesus Christ in the Thought and Writings of St. Francis* (St. Bonaventure NY: The Franciscan Institute, 1994), 70-76. For another text from Francis see *Earlier Rule* 23.8.

religious significance and challenge is the key to universalism and the starting point for penitential humanism. *Francis, his companions, and his listeners
are, in the first instance, humans.* Everyone in the city, rich and poor, old and
young, sick and healthy, Christian and non-Christian, is alive, a person, and
under God, a creature. All operate from within this same human zone of
existence; all belong.

Within this perspective, penitential humanism values human agency as a
means of participating in the creative activity of God. From the very beginning of his conversion Francis is led "to do penance" (*faciendi poenitentiam*),
"to do mercy" (*feci misericordiam*) and he extends an invitation to others to
engage in a similar project. "Doing," "making," "creating," "acting,"
"building," "following," "working": all are terms implying human agency
and freedom, engagement in a project which makes a person a true *imago
Dei*, made in the image of the one who is the Creator and the one who takes
up his cross in order to restore and re-create.[38] When Clare comes to follow
Francis, he uses the significant phrase: "Since by divine inspiration you have
made (*fecestis*) yourselves ...," and when counseling Leo he says: "In whatever way it seems best to you to please (*placere*) the Lord God and to follow
(*sequi*) His footprints and His poverty, do this (*faciatis*)...." In the *Later Rule*
(5.1) Francis refers to the "grace of working (*laborandi*)," an activity which
both he and Clare emphasize as constituent of the way of life (*Testament* 20;
Rule of Clare 7). "Labor" is exactly what Christ performed on this earth. (*4th
Letter to Agnes*, 22). The *Earlier Exhortation* uses variants of the term "to do"
as the key term linking its program of life: men and women "produce fruits
worthy of penance"; happy will they be when they "do these things and
persevere in doing them"; the Holy Spirit will "make His home" among
them; they are children of the heavenly Father "whose works they do." [39]

In addition to this focus on human agency in creation, the writings of
Francis and Clare contain numerous terms which imply "choice" (*voluntas*),
"freedom" (*discretio*), "reason" (*rationem*), and "reasonable" (*rationabile*).[40]
Giovanna Casagrande identifies all of these elements of working and
choosing as part of the model of life proposed to those influenced by the life

---

[38]For the images of God see Nguyen-Van-Kanh, *The Teacher of His Heart.*
[39]For background see Optato van Asseldonk, *Maria, Francesco e Chiara* (Rome: Istotito Is-
torico dei Cappuccini, 1989), 84-113.
[40]For word usage see Jean-Francois Godet et Georges Mailleux, *Corpus des Sources Fran-
ciscaines*, V, *Opuscula sancti Francisci, Scripta sanctae Clarae* (Louvain: CETEDOC, 1976).

and institutions of the commune. She refers to the penitential life as embodying a principle of *fare da se* which sanctifies the everyday world of work and the mechanical arts. Embedded in these notions is the reconciliation of the clerical and lay spheres of activity, the concept of a single religious culture open to the world.[41] What emerges from the entire complex of ideas is a new model of what it means to be "holy," one directly connected with the most basic elements of life: the city, the economy, work, behavior, participation in government.[42] Here was a penitential humanism designed to address the aspirations of the new society.

A Code of Behavior

Penitential humanism focuses on a common ethical project. Designed to address a fractious society torn by social, political, and religious dissent, the message of Francis and Clare places at the center of the Gospel and life a simple goal: the development of virtues and the avoidance of vice; the creation of a community of brothers and sisters; the proper use of power. Running throughout the writings of Francis and Clare is the primary call to embrace the Great Commandment: love of God, love of neighbor. The Earlier Exhortation begins, "All those who love the Lord *with their whole heart, with their whole soul and mind, with their whole strength* and love their neighbors as themselves," a phrase which Francis elaborated upon in his *Prayer Inspired by the Our Father* (vs. 5):

> *Your will be done on earth as in heaven:*
> That we may love you ...;
> And we may love our neighbor as ourselves
> By drawing them all to Your love with our whole strength,
> By rejoicing in the good of others as in our own,
> By suffering with others at their misfortunes,
> *And by giving offense to no one.*[43]

Elaborating on this most fundamental of commandments, Francis and Clare emphasize virtues and vices. Their basic social ethic includes: the

---

[41]Casagrande, *Religiosita Penitentziale*, 113-27. See also Flood, *Work for Everyone.*
[42]For the fullest elaboration see Jacques LeGoff, "Franciscanisme et Modèles Culturelles."
[43]See also *Earlier Rule* 23.8.

avoidance of slander, disputes, quarrelling, anger, murmuring, gossip, judgment, condemnation, noticing of defects, and, as Clare lists them, "pride,
vainglory, envy, greed, worldly care and anxiety, detracting and murmuring,
dissension and division." (*Earlier Rule* 11, *Later Rule* 10, *Rule of Clare* 10.4).
Positively, the friars are to encourage generosity, forgiveness, being "subject
to every human creature" (cf., for example, *Earlier Rule* 21.4-6, *Testament*
19). It is from within the context of the city, its problems and opportunities,
that one can read the *Salutation of the Virtues* and *Admonition XXVII*:

> Where there is charity and wisdom
> There is neither fear nor ignorance.
> Where there is patience and humility,
> There is neither anger nor disturbance.
> Where there is poverty with joy,
> There is neither covetousness nor avarice.
> Where there is inner peace and meditation,
> There is neither anxiousness nor dissipation.
> Where there is fear of the Lord to guard the house,
> There the enemy cannot gain entry.
> Where there is mercy and discernment
> There is neither excess nor hardness of heart.

The practice of this way of life is the embodiment of "being brother,
being sister," and the goal is the formation of a civic *fraternitas*, that most
fundamental of Franciscan values.[44] Included in the conception is the proper
use of power, a particularly relevant call to those who manage the city and
its institutions: "And let us love our neighbors as ourselves. And if anyone
does not want to love them as himself, let him at least not do them any
harm, but let him do good. Let whoever has received the power of judging
others pass judgment with mercy, as they would wish to receive mercy from
the Lord. For *judgment will be without mercy* for those *who have not shown
mercy.*" (*Later Admonition and Exhortation*, 26-29).

---

[44]This value of penitential humanism is so well known as hardly to need elaboration. For
placement in the context of the commune see Marie-Dominique Chenu, "Fraternias" Evangile
et condition socio-culturelle," *Revue Histoire de Spiritualite* 49 (1973): 385-400.

Religious Practices as Strategies of Enactment

Penitential humanism challenges its adherents to develop a "way of life," a *"politeia,"* a "methodology of evangelization" which promotes the fundamental values of the human community. The single term covering this appropriate "discipline of life" has traditionally been labeled "asceticism."[45] The American sociologist of religion Robert Wuthnow uses a more contemporary term, "religious practices" and notes that they have the following characteristics:

1. They are life-transforming, ending in service to others.

2. They occur in the midst of ordinary life and manifest a deliberate choice of communicating with God.

3. They involve not just external technique but are a response to one's deepest desires.

4. They are rewarding, producing a good way to life.

5. They are embedded in social institutions, follow a tradition, and are facilitated by belonging to a group.

6. They possess a moral dimension and engage one in the following of rules, a method with its own freedoms and constraints.

7. They involve deep reflection about one's own identity and develop around a core narrative which provides coherence and supplies an interpretative framework for life.[46]

It is in this framework of "religious practices" that the various instructions contained in Francis' writings can be re-interpreted so as to engage the life of the city.

Since the violence and unbelief cutting through the heart of the city also cuts through the hearts of those who live in it, Francis admonishes everyone to take care not to be trapped by the "cares and preoccupations" of the world" (*Rulers*, 2; *Earlier Exhortation*, 4-5; *Later Admonition and Exhortation*

---

[45]Numerous studies have reevaluated the interpretation of asceticism as a denial of worldly values and reframed it as a disciplined effort to develop a new social identity through bodily practices and symbols that give witness to fundamental beliefs. For significant background see David Brakke, *Athanasius and Asceticism* (Baltimore: Johns Hopkins University Press, 1995), especially on *politeia*; Kallistos Ware, "The Way of the Ascetics: Negative or Affirmative?" in Vincent L. Wimbush, Richard Valantasis, eds., *Asceticism* (New York: Oxford University Press, 1995), 3-15; Leif E. Vaage & Vincent L. Wimbush, eds., *Asceticism and the New Testament* (New York and London: Routledge, 1999).

[46]Wuthnow, *After Heaven, Spirituality in America Since the 1950's* (Berkeley: University of California Press, 1998), 168-98 on the contemporary turn to religious practices.

63-65; *Earlier Rule*, 22.20). He is well aware of the harsh requirements needed to break from the self constructed by society towards the self which is capable of the good life of penitential humanism. Remarkably similar instructions are given to the rulers of the people, to the lay penitents, and to the brothers. Some common disciplines of life, "therapies of the self-in-community," emerge as the best methods for promoting the new *politeia*:

1. the awareness of the day of death and the approaching judgment (*Rulers* 4; *Earlier Exhortation* 14-15; *Later Admonition and Exhortation* 82-85; *Earlier Rule* 21.7-8);

2. the reception of the body and blood of the Lord (*Rulers* 6; *EarlierExhoration* 3; *Later Admonition and Exhortation* 2; *Earlier Rule* 20.5-6; *Admonition* 1.8);

3. prayers of praise and thanks to the all powerful Lord God (*Rulers* 7; *Later Admonition and Exhortation* 61-62; *Earlier Rule* 21.2, 23);

4. confession of sins to each other and to the priest and the practice of reconciliation among people (*Later Admonition and Exhoration* 22, 26-28; *Earlier Rule* 21.5-6; 20.1-5);

5. fasting (*Later Admonition and Exhortation* 32; *Earlier Rule* 3.11-13);

6. visiting churches and respect for the clergy (*Later Admonition and Exhortation* 33; *Earlier Rule* 19.3, 20.4; *Testament* 4-6);

7. the necessity of doing penance or turning *ad Deum* (*Earlier Rule* 23.7).

These traditional ritual and ascetic practices in the context of the city are oriented to the formation of a new commonwealth of peoples, a new fraternity where everyone is brother and sister. They are necessary to break the hold of the internalized, sub-personal passions, which inhibit the freedom and agency of the person. These strategies of enactment are meant to produce human liberation for others. The rulers of the people have a public responsibility to foster this human way of life; the lay penitents are charged to focus it in the city; and the friars are the exemplars of what it means to incarnate it. But all of them, albeit with different positions and intensities, live so as to embody the same project under God of a penitential humanism.

Conclusion

It is very clear to the contemporary person that we no longer live within the context of a Christian world and that our dialogue with the city must engage the many different pluralisms of experience, belief, and responsibility found in our ministries. Certainly, today, not everyone in the city can be charged with the same *politeia*. However, all peoples face the common problems of how to build a civil community within a context of violence, poverty, and inhumanity; all peoples encounter the need for "therapies of the self-in-community" and "core narratives" which provide intellectual, emotional, and spiritual sustenance. Many of the contemporary strategies outlined earlier in this essay are attempts by the churches in the United States to bridge differences and articulate a philosophy of urban ministry which has wider appeal and which still marks a specifically religious contribution to society. It is a matter of religious institutions facing outwards towards the world in which they belong, articulating their own beliefs in such a way as to show their importance to human life as it is, and joining others in a common search for the promotion of the dignity of peoples. Although the spirituality which Francis of Assisi developed in the thirteenth century occurred in a markedly different and Christian context, still it is hoped that this re-reading of the sources in the light of the contemporary situation might enable brothers and sisters working in urban ministry to interpret the Gospel and the mission of the Church in such as a way as to create not an institutional ghetto but an "example and mirror for others" (St. Clare, *Testament* 6).

Joseph P. Chinnici, O.F.M., is currently academic dean of the Franciscan School of Theology, Berkeley, California, where he has been Professor of Church History since 1976. He served as Provincial Minister of the Province of Santa Barbara for nine years, and his most recent work in his specialty of the Catholic community in the United States is co-edited with Sister Angelyn Dries, O.S.F., *Prayer and Practice in the American Catholic Community* (Orbis, 2000). Joe has also written extensively on Franciscan themes; his most recent work is "Poverty: An Image for the Franciscan Presence in the World," *Laurentianum* 41 (2000), 413-37.

Questions for Reflection

1. How can we develop a common religious language about life commitments, disciplines, and ethical choices that unites the experience of the many different peoples who dwell in the city and are attracted by Franciscan institutions and groups? How do we emphasize our common human story and its Christian meaning in our preaching, our written word, and our ritual actions surrounding the passages of birth, marriage, and death? How do we relate this common human story with the life story of the "penitents from Assisi"?

2. "Penitential humanism" values life in this world and emphasizes creative participation in the work of a God who embraces all that is good. How do the participants in our institutions help shape an institution's vision, programs, and actions for the betterment of the people of the city? In what ways do our parochial programs point beyond themselves to the needs of the broader community? How does our social outreach share goals, programs, and resources with the other civic and religious participants in the life of the city?

3. Religious practices are disciplines which enact basic life values, embody core religious experiences, and foster perseverance and commitment. What types of prayers, devotions, ritual activities, and disciplines of life would help form an inner-city staff and community in a human, Christian, and Franciscan vision? How do we enact what we believe?

Heralding the Gospel in the Spirit of Francis: The Centrality of Preaching in Franciscan Urban Ministry

James A. Wallace, CSsR.

"The strength of the church is in communities of belief, values and mutually supportive action. Urban ministry that is not based on strong faith communities will be ephemeral or marginal."[1]

"Preaching constitutes the Church's first and fundamental way of serving the coming of the kingdom in individuals and in human society."[2]

Introduction

The reality we call *"the city"* frequently evokes an ambiguous response, even from those who would not choose to live anywhere else. It is the center of business and commerce, the hub of technology and communications, the home of the arts. More and more it is the desired place of habitation for the financially secure, with new condos and apartment buildings shooting up amid new convention centers and offices. But city lights and urban blight often coexist within a few blocks. The city is where the action - and the corruption - is. Sudden outbursts of violence can occur at any location, at any time, day or night. And it is the stage for most murders, robberies, random acts of violence, and tragic occurrences that could only take place with such frequency in this setting. To be concrete: over a few days in July, 1999, in Washington, D.C., two young girls, walking toward their residence in the early evening, were assaulted and robbed at knife-point; a grandmother was fatally shot in the back trying to get her grandchildren into the house; and an infant was the victim of ricocheting bullets aimed at his father.

The overall pattern is a familiar one: urban poverty breeds urban violence which in turn breeds urban decay and hopelessness. Daily the home-

---

[1]Frederick J. Perella, Jr., "Roman Catholic Approaches to Urban Ministry: 1945-85," in *Churches, Cities, and Human Community*, ed. Clifford J. Green (Grand Rapids: Eerdmans Publishing Co., 1996), 211.
[2]John Paul II, *The Mission of the Redeemer (Redemptoris Missio)*, #20.

less wander and beg, the physically and mentally ill are shoved from shelter to street, teens plan their funerals instead of their futures, the elderly spend their days barricaded behind bolted doors, and an increasing number of citizens purchase guns to protect themselves and their homes. Every Sunday at my local parish in the northeast section of the city, the names of those who have died by violence during the past week are read out as a petition in the Prayer of the Faithful; most are in their teens and twenties.

Death cuts off life far too early in the city. Still, every year, thousands continue to arrive there, some with high hopes, others in total desperation; it is the place of beginnings and of the second, as well as the last, chance. And among those who come to live in the city are men and women who have heard a call to be there to speak a word of life, a word that encourages and gives hope, calling citizens to community and mission. In short, they come to preach the good news of Jesus Christ, alive in our midst. We proclaim Jesus, Lord of heaven and earth, as one who dwells with us in the city.

The topic addressed here is the challenge of preaching within an urban setting and the abiding resources available to those who undertake this task, particularly as members of the Franciscan community or, perhaps, simply as admirers of this man who stands almost at the midpoint between Jesus and ourselves. The urban setting presents a particular challenge to the men and women who preach the gospel, week after week, in word and deed. To what end, preachers might sometimes ask? Does it do any good? Is it even conceivable that today's city can become the City of God, or, at least, a city for God? Can preaching really make a difference? Can the seed of God's Word be scattered to bring forth a harvest made visible in gospel-governed communities of faith, whose members go forth encouraged and determined to renew the face of the earth, to make their city a light shining on a hilltop, drawing others to it as a place "where we learn to celebrate the joy of humanity, where we learn that we are brothers and sisters regardless of our race, our religion, and our national origin"?[3]

To this end, three resources will be investigated: the Bible for its vision of the city, the Franciscan tradition for its vision of the preaching task, and the testimony of some of today's urban preachers for their perceptions of the challenges and changing reality of the city. Each area offers insight into the

---

[3]Andrew Young, "The City on the Hill, Reflections from a Former Mayor," *Interpretation* 54/1 (Jan. 2000): 54. The entire issue takes "The City" for its theme.

task of speaking a word of life and light in a setting too often identified with darkness and death. I will conclude with some final observations on urban preaching within Franciscan ministry, drawing on the contributions of the authors represented in this book.

Biblical Presentations of the City

"To be sure, the Bible does not offer a blueprint for urban restoration ...; it is not a how-to manual for overcoming racial prejudice and blighted housing. But scripture does disclose a compelling vision for the city...."[4]

I was momentarily surprised to read in a recent issue of the biblical journal *Interpretation* that, "contrary to popular opinion, the Bible has more to say about cities than it does about the countryside."[5] Like many others, I have tended to think of the biblical world as one primarily peopled by wandering nomads, searching shepherds, and a nation on the move, either out of or into slavery or exile; as a place of flowering fig trees, ripening vineyards, and falling manna; and a locus where all the important events took place out in the desert, down by the river, or up on the mountain top. But between Genesis and Revelation, the Bible offers a variety of images of the city. It is a place both of violence and victory, of misery and ministry, of corruption and conversion. Most importantly, it is a setting for faith and religious practice, a place where God comes to dwell with a people called to a covenantal relationship. What springs from the labor of Cain ultimately is imaged as the Bride coming down from the heavens.

According to Genesis, Cain was the founder of the first city, named for his son Enoch (Gen 4:17). The story of the tower of Babel (Gen 11) can be considered one of the first "tales of the city," vividly portraying human hubris in its attempt to create an urban culture apart from God. The "whole world" united in an attempt to build a city with a skyscraper, fulfilling their desire to "make a name for ourselves" (11:4). But God confused their language, scattering them over the earth, "and they stopped building the city." Later in Genesis, we hear of Sodom and Gomorrah, cities whose evil and

---

[4]William P. Brown and John T. Carroll, "The Garden and the Plaza: Biblical Images of the City," *Interpretation* 54/1 (Jan. 2000): 4.
[5]Brown and Carroll, 3.

wickedness were so great they were burnt to the ground (19:1-26). In the story of salvation history, Abram is led out of his native city Haran to wander through a new land (Gen 12:4); and Moses is addressed from a burning bush on God's holy mountain and sent from tending sheep to liberate the Israelites from Rameses, the city of Pharaoh, and take them out to the desert to meet their God (Ex 12:37). In the wilderness God woos a people and makes them his bride. From the early chapters of the Bible, God's preference for such outdoor settings as gardens, deserts, mountains, and star-filled skies do not indicate any affinity for Cain's creation.

Yet, in many other places in the Bible, the city is recognized as God's gift (Deut 6:10-12), as a setting for sustenance (Ps 107:4-9), a source for instruction (Is 2:3b-4),[6] and even for mass conversion (Jonah 1-4). And it is in a city that God decides to dwell, which brings us to the unique role of Jerusalem, both in its historical and theological significance in the Old and New Testaments. David's royal city, home of Solomon's Temple, becomes Zion in the writings of the prophets, signifying it as the city of Yahweh, the great king, who has chosen it as his permanent abode. Prophets like Isaiah (1:19-20), Micah (3:12), and Jeremiah (26:18-19) recognized the dangers of Jerusalem's pretensions to inviolability, and predicted that its citizens would be called to account. But even when the day of reckoning came and Jerusalem was destroyed and its people sent into exile, the prophets continued to proclaim the hope of its restoration with its walls being rebuilt and its Temple once more witnessing the return of the glory of Yahweh, and the city itself being a home to all nations (cf. Jer 30:18-19; Ez 5:5; 38:12; Is 40:1-2; 52:1,7-8). Jerusalem remains the focal point of the dreams of the nation, identified with the hope of the fulfillment of the Davidic messianic covenant.

Jerusalem continues to have theological significance in the New Testament. While Jesus enters first into the cities and towns of Galilee proclaiming the good news and later sends out his apostles and disciples to preach in the cities, it is to Jerusalem that he finally turns his face, and there fulfills his mission. In Luke's gospel especially, Jerusalem holds a central position as "the city of destiny for Jesus and the pivot for the salvation of all humankind."[7] Jesus weeps over Jerusalem as "the city that kills the prophets and stones those who are sent to it" and as the site whose enemies will "crush

---

[6]Brown and Carroll, 6-8.
[7]Joseph Fitzmyer, *Luke 1-9, Anchor Bible*. Quoted in *Anchor Bible Dictionary*, Vol. 3, "Jerusalem," by Philip King, 764.

you to the ground, you and your children within you, and they will not leave within you one stone upon another; because you did not recognize the time of your visitation from God" (Luke 13:34; 19:41-44).[8] Even so, Jerusalem's greatest significance lies ahead, for it is within this city that God's work of redemption in the dying and rising of Jesus will occur, and from this city salvation will flow forth to embrace the rest of the world. In a small room within the city, the risen Lord appears to the twelve (Luke 24:12ff; John 20:19ff). Acts presents the Holy Spirit, gift of the risen Lord, descending upon the disciples in Jerusalem (2:1-4), and propelling them out into the world. Peter preaches his first proclamation of Jesus as Lord and Messiah there (2:14-39), and from there the other disciples go forth to spread the gospel (Acts 8:4). Paul receives his commission to preach to the Gentiles in its Temple (Acts 22:17-21) and in his letter to the Romans, Paul recognizes Jerusalem as the location of the gospel's origin (15:19). Finally, in the book of Revelation, the new Jerusalem becomes the symbol of the kingdom of God which comes down out of heaven (3:12; 21:1-22:5), whereas Hebrews speaks of the heavenly Jerusalem to which the just ascend (12:22-24). Biblical scholar John L. McKenzie draws out a relevant implication of this final image when he writes: "The imagery of the heavenly city is a testimonial of the conviction that *it is in the life of the city that man (sic) reaches the highest fulfillment of his desires and powers. . . .*"[9] Jerusalem, then, while occupying a unique role in salvation history, also becomes a symbol of every city's potential under the grace of God.

The New Testament also witnesses to the early days of Christianity as an urban phenomenon.[10] Acts reminds us that not only did the preaching of Jesus as risen Lord begin in the city, but the earliest communities found a home in such cities as Antioch, Thessalonica, Ephesus, Philippi, Corinth, and Rome. In the cities of the region of Asia Minor, the word of God took root in the hearts of Jews and Gentiles. The city served as the home of the early church, and from the city Christianity moved out to become a faith embraced by all the nations.

---

[8]All quotations of the scriptures are taken from the *New Revised Standard Version* (Nashville: Thomas Nelson, 1989).

[9]John L. McKenzie, S.J., *Dictionary of the Bible*, "City" (Milwaukee: Bruce Publishing Co., 1965), 140. Italics mine.

[10]See Wayne A. Meeks' *The First Urban Christians, The Social World of the Apostle Paul* (New Haven: Yale University Press, 1983).

Thus, the biblical witness reminds us that the city is not only the habitation of humankind in its manifestations of arrogance, self-serving action, and the sinful neglect of those who are poor and defenseless, but also the dwelling place of God among us, a place where God works the divine will in the communities of faith that take root there. And Scripture calls us to an awareness in our own day that the city has the potential not only for impoverishing us, devouring our dreams, destroying our young, and ambushing our elderly; but also for being a place of ongoing possibility and achievement through the power of the Spirit, a setting for the kingdom of God to be glimpsed and experienced. As an expression of a kingdom that will come fully only at the end time, it nevertheless signals even now, in unexpected ways, that here is where God dwells with his holy people, here is holy ground.

From the city of man to the city of God, how does this transformation take place? One way is through the preaching of the gospel of Jesus Christ that bears fruit in a community of faith, a living out of a hope grounded in things unseen. St. Paul once asked an urban congregation he hardly knew: "... how are they to call on one in whom they have not believed. And how are they to hear without someone to proclaim him? And how are they to proclaim him unless they are sent?" (Rom 10:14-15). Faith binds together the Christian community in hope and love. And "faith comes from what is heard, and what is heard comes through the word of Christ" (Rom 10:17). This work of preaching the gospel of Jesus Christ, therefore, is at the heart of all urban ministry.[11] Preaching ministers to others by touching the lives of those it addresses, nourishing and enriching them.[12] It brings to hungry people the bread of life, that is, Jesus, the Word of God. And in so doing, it begins the transformation of wherever people of faith are living into the city where God dwells.

---

[11]The work of preaching has been given new emphasis since the Second Vatican Council and the restoration of the homily in *Sacrosanctum Concilium* (#35.2 and #52), along with various magisterial documents, such as Paul VI's *Evangelization in the Modern World* (1975) and John Paul IIs *Catechesis in our Time* (1979), and in such regional efforts as the NCCB-USCC document, *Fulfilled In Your Hearing* (1982).

[12]The *General Instruction of the Roman Missal* uses this image to describe the homily as "a necessary source of nourishment of the Christian life" (#41); see *The Sacramentary* (New York: Catholic Book Publishing Co., 1974), 25.

Urban Preaching in the Franciscan Tradition:
Heralding the Gospel

"All the brothers, under the leadership of the Holy Spirit, are sent to the whole world to be heralds of the Gospel." (1987 General Constitutions of the Friars Minor, Art. 83)

This statement identifying the Friars Minor as heralds of the gospel is certainly faithful to the mind of Francis and can be understood as the heart of a contemporary approach to preaching in an urban context. In our cities, the good news is to be proclaimed anew in every generation; the call to turn to the God revealed in Jesus Christ is to sound forth in a way that the children of a new millennium can hear and respond to it. In his *Letter to the Entire Order*, Francis wrote that "(the Son of God) has sent you into the entire world for this reason (cf. Tob 13:4) that in word and deed you may give witness to his voice and bring everyone to know that there is no one who is all powerful except Him (Tob 13:4)."[13] Dominic Monti, a Franciscan church historian, expresses it succinctly when he writes: "the Franciscan charism is essentially missionary in character."[14] What implication does that have for today's friars working in cities? It grounds the preaching task in a particular understanding of the preacher as an evangelizer.

Drawing on the Franciscan tradition and recent Franciscan writings, I would suggest three characteristics of early Franciscan preaching that remain relevant today: 1) an emphasis on knowing and living the Scriptures; 2) the cultivation of an appropriate speaking style that reaches the listeners in their life situation; and 3) the projection of a vision calling believers to involvement and action.

The Centrality of Scripture. The Legend of Perugia[15] speaks of Francis taking a broom on his preaching tours, and, when he came into a dirty church, he would clean it. But it was not only respect for the presence of the

---

[13]*Francis and Clare: The Complete Works* (hereafter, *CW*), translation and introduction by Regis Armstrong, O.F.M. Cap. and Ignatius C. Brady, O.F.M. (Mahwah, N.J.: Paulist Press, 1982), 56.

[14]Dominic Monti, "Franciscan Ministry: Changing Contexts and Historical Developments," *The Cord*, 41/3 (March, 1991): 69. Similarly, the *Dizionario Francescano* claims that the friars minor are the first missionary order in the church.

[15]Editor's note: the newest edition of Franciscan Sources no longer uses this name, but calls the text the Assisi Compilation.

Lord in the Eucharist that concerned him. In his *Letter to the Clergy*, after first rebuking those responsible for leaving the Body and Blood of Christ in an unclean place, he demands that "wherever the written words of the Lord may be found in unbecoming places, they are to be collected and kept in a place that is becoming."[16] The medievalist Daniel Lesnick observes that for Francis the Bible was not simply a source of information about God but an actual presence,[17] and he called on his friars and other clergy to reverence it accordingly. The experiential power of the Scriptures is rooted in Francis' own call: it was hearing the gospel's missionary discourse (Matt 10:5-42) during Mass at the Porziuncola that moved him to take up the life of an itinerant preacher.[18] The gospel of Jesus Christ was his life and it was to be central to the lives of those who would join him: "I am obliged to serve all and minister to them the sweet words of my Lord."[19] While we find ample testimony of Francis' love for Scripture, he cautioned his friars that it was not enough to be familiar with the words and how to interpret them to others; rather, only those who follow the spirit of sacred Scripture receive life from it.[20] This stress on getting beyond understanding the message of Scripture to living out of the mystery of Christ occurs again and again in his writings (see the *Earlier Rule*: XVII, and *Later Rule*: I).

Christ was at the center of Scripture, and in the life of Francis we find a total identification with the mysteries of his birth, suffering and death, and presence in the Eucharist. At the heart of Francis' preaching was the person of Jesus: "Blessed is that religious who takes no pleasure and joy except in the most holy words and deeds of the Lord." (*Admonition* XX) Again, Lesnick sees that for Francis and his followers, "the active remembrance of Christ became the motor of the spiritual life."[21] Love of the Scriptures continued as a Franciscan hallmark in followers like Anthony,[22] Bonaventure,

---

[16]*CW, Letter to the Clergy* 50. This same admonition is given to his own: See *Letter to the Custodians* 53.

[17]Daniel R. Lesnick, *Preaching in Medieval Florence: The Social World of Franciscan and Dominican Spirituality* (Athens, GA: University of Georgia Press, 1989), 139.

[18]Charles V. Finnegan, OFM, "Franciscans and the 'New Evangelization'- I," *The Cord*, 41/1 (Jan., 1991): 5. This is the first of a series of six articles written on Franciscan evangelization by Finnegan for *The Cord* during 1991.

[19]Finnegan, I: 7.

[20]*CW, Admonition* VII: 30.

[21]Lesnick, 139.

[22]Anthony was called the "ark of the New and Old Testament" by Gregory IX because of his exhaustive knowledge of Scripture; as a teacher he insisted on a thorough knowledge of Scripture on the part of his charges. He writes: "Just as gold excels all other metals in excellence, so does the knowledge of Sacred Scripture surpass all other forms of knowledge. He who

and Bernardine of Siena, to name a few whose preaching was noted for its biblical foundations. This desire for greater understanding of the Scriptures was one of the bonds between the early Franciscans and their listeners. Monti notes that "the literate population of the time hungered to approach Scripture on its own or at least through effective preaching," recognizing it as a vehicle for a deeper relationship between the individual and God.[23]

Is the hunger any less now? Is that hunger being met? The liturgical reform that brought a new lectionary into being was only one step in making available the rich nourishment to be found at the table of the Word. Even while the Lectionary offers a greater number and variety of biblical texts, stretching over the three-year Sunday cycle and two-year daily cycle, still I would suggest that much of the Bible remains unheard by and unfamiliar to many people. And a new lectionary alone does not satisfy the hunger to meet the God who communicates to us through the biblical word. There remains a need of cultivating in today's preachers a deeper understanding and love of Scripture. An evaluative study of almost one hundred homilies given by over thirty preachers was conducted recently by Barbara Reid, O.P., and Leslie Hoppe, O.F.M., members of the Biblical Studies department at the Catholic Theological Union in Chicago. Their assessment was that almost three-fourths of the homilies studied "did not reflect sound exegetical preparation and informed theological reflection"; therefore, the homilies themselves "were not the product of sound biblical interpretation."[24] The voice of Francis urging his community to recognize the centrality of Scriptures in the work of ministry, both within and beyond the liturgical life of the church, is a needed corrective in the present.

Not By Words Alone. For Francis, the words of preaching were to flow out of one's life; of themselves, words were recognized as instrumental, serving as a bridge that connected people, but not to be greatly fussed over. He even appears to be suspicious of words in and of themselves. Francis described himself as "ineloquent" and not used to public speaking. Thomas of Spalato, who heard him preach in Bologna in 1222, recorded that, while his

---

does not know Sacred Scripture possesses no knowledge." It is no wonder Pius XII gave him the title *Doctor Evangelicus* when he was declared a doctor of the church. See Claude Jarmak, O.F.M. Conv., *If You Seek Miracles: Reflections of St. Anthony of Padua* (Padua: Edizioni Messaggero, 1998), 16.

[23]Monti, 73.

[24]Barbara E. Reid, O.P. and Leslie J. Hoppe, O.F.M., *Preaching from the Scriptures: New Directions for Preparing Preachers* (Chicago: Catholic Theological Union, 1998).

manner and clarity of expression were impressive, he was not possessed with a "sacred eloquence."[25] Perhaps his lack of a university education played a part, but an intuitive wisdom could also have made him suspicious, recognizing that words could easily become a terminus of desire rather than serve as a stimulus for action: "For the spirit of the flesh desires and is most eager to have words, but (cares) little to carry them out" (*Earlier Rule*: XVII). He also reminded his friars of the importance of preaching by their actions: "We are therefore to go through the world exhorting all men and women more by our examples than by our words."[26]

Nevertheless, language was a primary vehicle to address the new audience to be found where Francis and his followers preached. From the beginning, Franciscan preaching was rooted in the city life of its day and life in the city was changing. Francis and his "lesser brothers" preached to a newly emerging class of people, the townsfolk of the rising urban centers like Assisi, Florence, Siena and Bologna. It was their task and challenge to address an audience that included the new class of merchants, artisans, and shopkeepers.[27] This was a group to whom words had not been kind. Gratian's *Decretum* declared that "a merchant is rarely or ever able to please God," while theologian Peter Lombard taught that merchants could not perform their work without sinning; and money lending was declared immoral if any profit was made.[28] The friars came from this class of people and were able to communicate with them, using the language and imagery of commerce and everyday experience in the marketplace.

To a people looking for moral guidance in living out their state of life, the friars preached in a way that nourished their spirit, holding up to them the possibility of living a devout life: "a Christian life of prayer and sacrifice not modeled upon that of monks or dependent upon the vicarious merits acquired for them by professional ascetics, but one lived fully in the

---

[25]Seamus Mulholland, O.F.M., "The Power of St. Francis' Preaching, *The Cord*, 38/4 ((April, 1988): 102-103. The author also quotes Francis' saying, " . . . I am a worthless religious, I have no education and I am inexperienced in speaking. I have received the gift of prayer rather than that of preaching . . . " (103).

[26]Finnegan, I: 7. Cf. *Earlier Rule*: XVII. 3.

[27]Lesnick distinguishes between the audiences for Franciscan and Dominican preaching. He links the Dominicans with the *popolo grasso*, or the merchants and bankers, and the Franciscans with the *popolo*, or humbler class of artisans, craftsmen, shopkeepers, and professionals. See *Preaching in Medieval Florence*, Chapters 1, 2, 6, and 7.

[28]Monti, 76.

world."[29] The form this preaching took was the *sermo humilis* unique to the Franciscan friars, a style of preaching that appealed to the emotions and the imagination, distinct from the *sermo modernus*, a style cultivated by the Dominicans, which appealed to the intellect. The former led to action for the sake of others, the latter to self-control and social dominance.[30]

Like other reformers, Francis called on his brothers to preach in words that were "well chosen and chaste, for the instruction and edification of the people, speaking to them of vices and virtues, punishment and glory in a discourse that is brief, because it was in few words that the Lord preached while on earth" (*Later Rule*: IX). The style of the friars was characterized as concrete, using narratives and anecdotes, employing books of *Exempla* drawn from the lives of the saints,[31] the natural world, and the everyday life experience of the listeners. Preaching was aimed at evoking the memory of the story of Jesus so as to participate in it. It attempted to arouse the imagination, excite the emotions, touch the heart, and stir the listeners to inner transformation and action in the world. Francis thought of such preaching as "an always new and unpredictable game."[32] It flowed "*ex abundantia cordis*" and was marked by spontaneity rather than the scholarship of the scholastic university sermon, although later eminent Franciscans would make use of the latter's complex structure as a scaffolding on which to hang their stories and imaginative expression. Because of the preaching of the friars, the newly emergent middle class found in the gospel a persuasive word that addressed their lives, both challenging and comforting them.

A Transforming Vision. Francis is said to have begun his sermons with the words, "The Lord give you peace."[33] His preaching presented and invited others into a world of reconciliation. Several narratives from the life of Francis capture the transformation his preaching could effect: the reconciliation between the wolf and the people of Gubbio; the mutual respect to be found between Francis and the Moslem Sultan when they met at Dami-

---

[29]C.H. Lawrence, *The Friars: The Impact of the Early Mendicant Movement on Western Society* (London: Longman, 1994), 121.

[30]Lesnick, Chapters VI and VII.

[31]For a treatment of the role of the saints in preaching as part of a "culture of devotion" which contributed to "the perception of the city as the place where the holy dwelt," see Peter Howard's "The Preacher and the Holy in Renaissance Florence," in *Models of Holiness in Medieval Sermons* (Louvain: Federation Intern des Instituts d'Etudes Medievales, 1996), 355-70.

[32]Lesnick, 138.

[33]Anscar Zawart, O.F.M.Cap., *The History of Franciscan Preaching and of Franciscan Preachers 1209-1927* (New York: Wagner, 1927), 263.

etta in Egypt; the restoration of peace among the various local factions when the demons of war were exorcised by his preaching in the city of Arezzo. These instances present Francis as peacemaker. While we often associate him either with the Christ of the incarnation or the passion due to his building the first crèche and his bearing of the stigmata, another profound connection with the mystery of Christ is between Francis and the risen Lord, whose first gift to his followers was peace (cf. John 20: 19-21). These stories of Francis leave us with a vision of peace that can bind us with nature, our neighbors, and those whose faith differs from ours.

Early Franciscan preaching addressed people whose cities were wracked by warfare without and feuds within. The moral exhortations of the friars aimed at bringing peace to these cities and towns, rather than revolutionary change. Such preaching did more than call for an end to urban violence; it held out the possibility of interior peace within each person and between members of the various social classes, by providing a way of seeing themselves in communion with God and each other. DaCampagnola observes that the Gospel Francis preached was not asocial or hostile to the world like that of the Cathari or the Spirituals, but it "helped bring about a greater social realism in his age."[34] The preaching of the friars addressed and embraced the middle class and the marginalized, and it confronted both the politically and the religiously powerful by courageously naming three social evils that prevented people from living in peace and harmony: an obsessive desire for riches, power, and knowledge. It modeled an alternative way of living, to be embodied in the daily lives of the friars, this being the strongest sermon of all.

In his writings, Francis employs a number of key words in describing the community of friars, words such as *service, peace, humility, simplicity, poverty*, and, above all, *charity*, indicating the characteristics of this new family who were to model an alternative way of living the gospel. The evangelization of Francis and his "lesser brothers" was above all incarnational.

Francis reminds us of the need to rediscover for our own time the basic message of the gospel and to find a way of preaching that moves others to become involved in God's plan of personal reconciliation and social transformation. His own preaching provided a new heralding of the good news

---

[34]Stanislaus da Campagnola, Francis of Assisi and the Social Problems of his Time," *Greyfriars Review* 2 (1988): 139.

and a practical program of bringing about a commitment to penance and peace. Francis' genius lay in being able to preach to all the people of his time, rich and poor, Christian and non-Christian. The final purpose of this preaching has been described as having hearers "confront God's presence in experience and to move them to conversion of heart and to action and involvement."[35] John Paul II provided a fitting tribute and a challenge to his contemporary followers by describing Francis as one who "wrote the gospel of Christ in the hearts of the people of his time . . . (and) carried in his own heart the misfortunes and concerns of his contemporaries."[36] This is a major ongoing task in our day, especially in the urban setting.

Urban Preaching Today: Proclaiming the Gospel to the Nations

A third component for consideration is the present experience of urban preaching. I have consulted an experienced group of preachers presently or formerly involved in urban ministry, inquiring about their preaching.[37] Their reflections pertain to liturgical preaching. I will divide their comments into three sections: 1) the soul of city preaching; 2) the sound of city preaching; and 3) the challenge of city preaching. Two areas are noteworthy for helping preachers to meet this challenge.

The Soul of City Preaching. The soul of preaching is located in the gospel message proclaimed, in helping listeners to hear the good news and respond to it. "Is there any particular message or aspect of the gospel you find yourself preaching again and again?" is the first question I asked a group of preachers working in parishes in several cities on the east coast, including Washington, Baltimore, Philadelphia, New York, and Boston. The answers varied: "God's unconditional love," "the need for forgiveness and healing possible through Christ," "the importance of community," "speaking a word

---

[35]Finnegan, "Evangelization IV-Preaching," *The Cord* 41/7, (July-August, 1991): 219.

[36]Finnegan, I: 6.

[37]I have interviewed a group of seven priests, four religious and three diocesan, whose ministry in the inner city has averaged between 25-30 years, with two exceptions: one who had worked over twenty years in Paraguay until five years ago, and one who has only recently returned to inner city work after thirty years in suburban parishes. I asked them about the content and style of their preaching, how it would be different if they were preaching in a rural or suburban parish, and whether they saw the preaching of religious clergy making a distinct contribution. I am grateful to Msgr. Richard Burton, Msgr. Raymond East, James Gilmour, C.Ss.R., Msgr. Ray Kemp, Kevin Milton, C.Ss.R., Francis Skelly, C.Ss.R., Joseph Tizio, C.Ss.R.

that gives hope," "bringing the people a sense of Jesus' presence in their lives." One response focused particularly on the needs of parents: "City people are concerned about their kids, about handing on the meaning and values their faith has given them. They are also interested in two areas: how to pray and the importance of acknowledging sin and working for reconciliation." Two preachers spoke of the importance of moving their people from "a parochialism that is the institutional form of individualism" to a broader faith vision: "from Jesus and me to Us," and "from the sanctuary to the city." Another noted that his basic message has two parts: "God loves you-now, get involved."

The content of preaching is conditioned by the need for God's people to hear the basic proclamation of the good news of Jesus Christ, to know the reality of the church as the body of Christ whose members are gifted by the Spirit for the sake of the common good, and to instill an awareness of the mission of the church to the world. Each preacher interviewed saw the power of preaching resting in the strong proclamation of the Word of God, of God's definitive action in the person of Jesus and his saving death and resurrection, of God's ongoing work through the power of the Holy Spirit, and in bringing this home to the world in which their people live, so that the community of believers can act out of an awareness of God's love and life working in and through them to serve those in need, to transform the social structures needing change, and to further the coming of the kingdom of God.

The Sound of City Preaching. A preacher recently returning to inner city ministry after a long absence remarked, "I need to develop an inner city flavor in my homilies." All the preachers remarked on the importance of a certain style of preaching being more suitable for city ministry. One said that he has been strongly influenced by storefront preaching and preaching in the Baptist tradition, preaching that is more emotional and free. A Washington-based preacher expanded on this when he noted that "urban preaching for the last fifty years has for the most part been black preaching; that's mostly who has lived in the city. And for city preaching to be effective it must be both *content* rich and *context* rich." By the latter was meant a certain sound, rhythm, cadence, color. This same preacher spoke of the "preacher's toolbox" indicating that urban preachers in the African-American community need certain "tools" such as "stories, poetry, the King James version of the Bible, the words of hymns and spirituals – and the

Washington-based preacher expanded on this when he noted that "urban preaching for the last fifty years has for the most part been black preaching; that's mostly who has lived in the city. And for city preaching to be effective it must be both *content* rich and *context* rich." By the latter was meant a certain sound, rhythm, cadence, color. This same preacher spoke of the "preacher's toolbox" indicating that urban preachers in the African American community need certain "tools" such as "stories, poetry, the King James version of the Bible, the words of hymns and spirituals – and the melodies." The preachers who work in predominantly Hispanic parishes also noted the importance of preaching with a certain style that is more expressive, imaginative, dialogical, involving the people by asking questions.

The Challenge of City Preaching. There is a shift happening in many large cities. Whereas in the 19th century city preaching was most often directed to immigrants arriving from Europe, in the latter half of the 20th century, city preaching in the Catholic churches was varied but still fairly monolithic in composition, sometimes addressing a community composed of these same immigrants' descendants, or a predominantly Hispanic or African-American congregation, or sometimes an uneasy mix of two of these groups. The new millennium offers preachers a possibly greater challenge. Many urban preachers now look out at congregations that reflect a level of diversity never before experienced. Among those present might be blacks of various cultural traditions (African Americans, Caribbean blacks, Haitians, and Africans), Hispanics of various cultural traditions (Puerto Ricans, Dominicans, Cubans, Mexicans, Central Americans, and South Americans), and Asians of various cultural traditions (Koreans, Filipinos, Hmong, Vietnamese, Thai, and Chinese.) All the more urgent is the preachers' need to have knowledge of the various cultural groups, their customs and values, the experiences that have brought them to this church and their expectations.

Preachers must be responsible for knowing three stories: the story of God contained in the Scriptures, the story of the parish they are working in, and the story of the different peoples they address, both as distinct cultural groups and as individuals with their own unique histories. One preacher noted that although there are some universal "plots" that characterize urban life (for instance, "Loved and lost," "Been to hell's kitchen and licked all the pots," "Blessed in spite of my sins"), a good preacher needs to spend time knowing as many people as possible, for each person's story is uniquely his/her own. And then preachers must know how to speak with the commu-

Another challenge involves the preacher's knowing which "voice" is most beneficial to the community at a particular time. Contemporary homileticians have written of four such "voices": the *herald*, who proclaims the initial gospel message of good news and the call to conversion; the *teacher*, who uses the biblical text to expound on the sacred mysteries and the guiding principles of the Christian life; the *witness* who offers his or her own testimony to the power of God revealed in Jesus Christ through the Spirit; and the *interpreter*, who mediates meaning by offering a biblical interpretation of human existence which enables a community to recognize God's presence and respond to that presence through the act of Eucharist and a life lived in conformity with the gospel.[38] Whichever voice is decided on, Bishop Ken Untener reminds preachers: "when preparing a homily we participate in the same action of the Spirit that formed the scriptural text itself."[39] Through the efforts of preachers open to the Holy Spirit, God's Word continues to be spoken anew.

Urban Preaching in a Franciscan Key

The preachers consulted in preparing the preceding section unanimously affirmed that preachers from religious communities offer a unique perspective when they preached out of their respective charisms. The basic melody might be the same; but each religious community plays it in a distinct key. An approach to Franciscan urban preaching today can draw on both its past and the present in charting its future. While the origins of Franciscan preaching remind us of certain important values, so, too, do the various contemporary perspectives on Franciscan urban ministry offered in this volume, serving to complement the historical tradition of Franciscan preaching through an extension of this tradition's values and emphases.

First, the early Franciscans were lay preachers, their members sent forth to proclaim the gospel by word and deed in the marketplace. Both aspects have relevance for our day. From the very beginning of Christianity,

---

[38]All four images of preaching are biblically grounded and have been supported in various ecclesial documents since the time of the Second Vatican Council. See Robert P. Waznak, *An Introduction to the Homily* (Collegeville: Liturgical Press, 1998) for a thorough treatment of all four models of the preacher, 31-71. See also James A. Wallace, *Imaginal Preaching: An Archetypal Perspective* (Mahwah: Paulist Press, 1995), 10-15.

[39]Ken Untener, *Preaching Better: Practical Suggestions for Homilists* (Mahwah: Paulist Press, 1999), 7.

preaching was rooted in the experience of ordinary men and women, not clerical or monastic experience. From Peter and Magdalene to Francis and his followers, the laity was given the gift of being called to proclaim the mystery of Christ. With more and more laity today enrolling in schools of ministry and receiving a theological education and even some degree of initial formation in preaching, it is the religious communities that can provide the opportunity for these voices to be heard. With the present restrictions on preaching the homily during the Eucharist, the opportunity for lay preaching can be extremely limited in the normal liturgical life of most communities. But the Franciscan tradition of preaching in other venues can be taken up in ways that have been part of their tradition but also unique to our time. Teams of clerical, religious, and lay preachers might be formed to speak not only on such occasions as parish retreats or missions, but also within other settings: from early morning talks in the boardrooms of business firms on particular issues of theology, to evening catechetical instructions in local pubs (the "Theology on Tap" series popular in many cities), to witnessing in the world of cyberspace by entry into chat rooms where religion and spirituality attract interested seekers. For Francis the town marketplace was where he and his followers engaged the merchants and artisans; today's urban context offers an unlimited number of possibilities, circumscribed only by our limited imagination and faltering courage.

Beyond the challenge provided by the Franciscan past, the articles contained in this work contribute to a profile of Franciscan preaching in the contemporary urban context. Two constructs in particular offer a foundation for preaching today in a "Franciscan key": the necessity of having and maintaining a "critical distance" (Monti) while addressing contemporary urban dwellers, and the need to ground preaching in a "penitential humanism" (Chinnici). The foci of the other contributors will be related to these two headings.

Franciscan preaching needs to maintain a "critical distance" on urban life in order to name both its demons and its blessings. This is very much in line with the role of the preacher as an interpreter of life, helping the community to recognize both the movement of God in their midst and those aspects of life in which the powers and principalities have yet to totally yield their ground. The interpreter has also been called a "mediator of meaning," one who stands in the middle, in the "between," reflecting a certain distance between both the world of the scriptures where preachers are called to "dwell" in silence, study, and prayer, and the world of the community today where the preachers spend most of their lives listening to the dreams, fears, joys and sorrows of their people. Both worlds must be investigated as part of preaching preparation, but it is by maintaining a critical distance in both that the preacher is able to correlate how each sheds light on the other. Critical judgment allows one to name the blessings and curses, the angels and demons of modern life. Critical distance enables a preacher to offer a "transformative vision" as an alternate vision to those society offers. Keefe's emphasis on providing an "alternate vision" of society grounded in conversion, poverty, minority, and contemplation is a Franciscan response to the awareness that people live according to various "scripts" and preaching's goal is to offer a *gospel* script that corresponds to the challenges of contemporary life in the urban setting. [40]

Furthermore, a critical distance from what presently passes for justice enables preachers to propose the alternate model of "restorative justice" (Johnson), attending not only to the offender, but to the needs of victim, offender, and community. The focus of restorative justice is "people, not procedures" with a goal of healing both the victims and the perpetrators. To restore the community to wholeness is the end of restorative justice, to see that nothing that has been entrusted to us will be lost. To maintain this view on those who have done terrible things to innocent bystanders calls for a critical distance.

How to achieve this "critical distance" is the challenge. This depends a great deal on the working of the Holy Spirit. And for the Holy Spirit to be part of the process, the preacher must attend to his/her spiritual life. John Westerhoff offers preachers some practical thoughts on this in his *Spiritual Life; The Foundation for Preaching and Teaching*, addressing the loss of energy so many preachers experience as being rooted in the erosion and ignoring of their spiritual lives. [41]

Finally, there is the grounding Chinnici's "penitential humanism" offers to preachers by fostering the recognition that all people are gifted by God

---

[40]See also Walter Brüggemann, *Cadences of Home: Preaching among Exiles* (Louisville: Westminster John Knox, 1997), especially Chapter 3: 24-37.

[41]John Westerhoff, *Spiritual Life: The Foundation for Preaching and Teaching* (Louisville: Westminster John Knox, 1994), xi.

with a capacity to take part in the ongoing work of creation. "Penitential humanism" as described provides both a lens on the world that is biblically grounded in the dignity of all people and a program for empowerment rooted in the cultivation of a virtuous life supported by Christian praxis. This "global vision" embraces all men and women, and all creation, as the poor man of Assisi did. Transformation has been a hallmark of the Franciscan story from the beginning; its representative narratives speak to the human capacity to embrace what has been declared "unclean," to convert what has been experienced as deadly, to converse with what was perceived as fearsome and life-threatening, and to cast out what is truly evil so as to redeem and restore what was created as "very good." Lepers and wolves, warriors and demons, have not ceased to come into our lives. Penitential humanism helps us to know them in spirit and in truth.

Although offered to those who work in the area of social services, Margraf's "strengths perspective" reminds preachers that the view from the pulpit must include a capacity to see a community's inner strength at all times. Diagnosing the spiritual sickness of any situation must not exclude operating in the awareness that the gifts of the Spirit are also at work in all involved. And Carroll's call to participate in the dream of racial harmony is a universal summons with no less an urgency today, indeed all the more urgent in the face of the new outbreaks of genocide that continue to plague our world. All preaching must lead to a stronger commitment to the eschatological goal of all God's children gathering at a table in the kingdom to feast forever. Preaching in the spirit of Francis today is a preaching whose primary concern is the transformation of the city of man into the city of God, enabling all people to come together even now as true children of God, empowered to live lives of justice, peace, healing, and communion.

Conclusion

Franciscan preaching has had two goals from the beginning: the promotion of God's glory and the building up of the body of Christ. Francis recognized this task as rooted solidly in the work of the Holy Spirit, calling his preachers to be animated by this same Spirit who enables us to speak a word of life. Not matter how threatening the city may sometimes appear, it is called to house the presence of God and become a dwelling place of the Divine Mystery. Preaching is one of the primary instruments for bringing this about. In our own day it will fulfill its task when it offers today's citizens a sense of their identity in Christ, forming every individual and each group into a community that knows itself as his body, and inspires in this body a sense of missionary endeavor, to go forth from the table to transform the neighborhood, the district, the entire urban area, but most especially those corners and crevices where those who are poor and needy are confined and often forgotten.

There is a mosaic of St. Anthony at the Franciscan Shrine in Boston that has the saint standing before a group of people of all ages and walks of life. In his left hand he holds fire and is gazing intently upon it. Such is the task of all those who join in the work of the God whose first words at creation were, "Let there be light," and whose Word become flesh told us, "I have come to cast fire on the earth." Anthony stands gazing intently at the fire as all preachers of the word must do, attentive to it, striving to make its meaning available to all who wait on its power to bring light, warmth, and healing. It is this Word that brings us together and shapes us into the Body of Christ; it is this Word that sends us out into the world's towns and cities. May the spirit of Francis continue to guide us in this good work of God known as preaching the gospel of Jesus Christ.

James A. Wallace, C.Ss.R., is Professor of Homiletics at the Washington Theological Union, Washington, D.C. His recent publications include *Preaching to the Hungers of the Heart* (Liturgical Press, 2002), and *Witnessing the Holy Land: A Pilgrimage in Image and Word*, with artist Ellouise Schoettler (Mahwah, New Jersey: Paulist Press, 1999).

Questions for Reflection

1. What has been your experience of the city where you minister? What is *your* vision of what it can be? How do the Scriptures contribute to this vision?

2. How does the Franciscan charism for preaching the Gospel actually influence your preaching? How do you see yourself continuing in the Franciscan tradition of preaching?

3. Who are your listeners (i.e., their cultural backgrounds, customs, rituals) that make up your congregation when you preach? What are the "languages" you need to know in order to speak to their experience, concerns, and hopes?

4. What aspect of the gospel is most important for your community to hear? Are there certain biblical themes and values you find at the heart of your preaching?

5. Which of the perspectives offered within the other articles in this volume do you find helpful for a contemporary approach to preaching out of the Franciscan charism?

Integration Questions for Further Reflection

We offer the following questions on issues that are common to these ministries. As each of the above articles contains material that converges with themes found in the other articles, in order to help focus and integrate your reflection we have indicated at the end of each question the Chapter (article) numbers that correlate with the issue.

1. Liturgical celebration is central to the life of any Christian community. What role does liturgy play in an/your urban ministerial setting? What are some of the unique characteristics of liturgical life in an urban setting? (cf. chapters 2, 6, 7)

2. Frequently, urban ministries are characterized by alliances with outside groups (e.g., other religious organizations, inter-faith/ecumenical activities, civic groups, government organizations, social service agencies, business organizations, etc.). How does this enable an urban ministry to accomplish its goals effectively? What are some of the challenges associated with this kind of activity? In your experience, what affiliations have been most helpful? (cf. chapters 2, 3, 6)

3. Urban ministries, by definition, are located within cities. What are some of the particularities of an/your urban setting? What are some of the blessings specific to ministry in an urban center? What are the challenges that the/your contemporary city offers to people/you who engage in urban ministry? (cf. chapters 4, 7)

4. By its nature, urban ministry is an ambiguous undertaking. Often, "successes" seem thin and challenges are myriad. What are some of the ambiguities that are inherent in an/your urban ministry setting? What kinds of things enable a person/you to acknowledge the ambiguity of an

urban ministerial setting and learn to live with it? (cf. chapters 1, 2, 4, 5, 6, 7)

5. A person in an urban ministerial setting is often required to take risks in addressing a very complex set of issues. What are some of the risks involved in an/your urban ministry? What are some of the things that enable a person/you to step up and meet the challenges of the day? What are some of the support systems (institutional and non-institutional) available to the person/you who ministers in a city? (cf. chapters 1, 2, 3, 4, 5, 6)

6. Typically, ministry in an urban setting requires a special sensitivity to a variety of challenging ethical situations. What are some of those challenges? What tools are available for the person/you in urban ministry to more carefully discern the relevant ethical issues and appropriate responses? (cf. chapters 1, 2, 3, 4, 5, 6)